In memory of Orval George Pall,
November 22, 1951 – June 6, 1986
who loved and cherished our wild lands

Eastern Slopes Wildlands
Our Living Heritage

A Proposal from
The Alberta Wilderness Association

ISBN 0-920074-05-7

Printed and bound in Canada.

Copyright © 1986 The Alberta Wilderness Association

Front cover photograph by Neil Erkamp

Back cover photographs by Cheryl Bradley, R.P. Pharis

Contributing authors   Cheryl Bradley, Lee Christie, John Eisenhauer, Ross Goodwin, Bozena Kolar, Dianne Pachal, Vivian Pharis, Alf Skrastins, Don Wales.

Researchers   Mike Judd, Barb Kruger, Dave McNeil, James Tweedie, Kathy Wilkinson, Farley Wuth.

Photographers   Cheryl Bradley, Robert Carroll, Neil Erkamp, Halle Flygare, Glenbow Museum, William Michalsky, Dianne Pachal, Orval Pall, Parks Canada, Vivian & Dick Pharis, Dave Shackleton, Don Wales, Cleve Wershler, Cliff Wallis.

Editors   Bozena Kolar, Al Brawn.

Project Manager   Bozena Kolar

Typing   Pam Davis, Sharon Coupal, Joan LaChance.

Cartographer   Marta Styk

Preparation for lithography   D. Scollard

Typesetter   Phyllis Hall

Acknowledgements

The Alberta Wilderness Association gratefully acknowledges the financial support of the Canada Employment Program, The Alberta Recreation, Parks and Wildlife Foundation, the Canadian Petroleum Association, Petro-Canada, Mike and Diane McIvor.

The Alberta Wilderness Association also gratefully acknowledges the assistance with technical information provided by Alberta Culture, Alberta Fish and Wildlife, Alberta Forest Service, Alberta Public Land Division, Alberta Recreation and Parks, Chester B. Beaty and Hugh Dempsey.

Contents

Wildlands of the Eastern Slopes

Even before opening my eyes I knew what to expect. The early morning light filtered through the tent flap. A bird whose call I didn't recognize warned intruders to stay away from his territory. I could smell the mountain air and taste the coolness of the morning. Content, I cuddled deeper into my sleeping bag. Curled against me, my daughter made small sounds in her sleep. I would be rising soon, leaving the tent to start the fire and perk that ever-welcome first cup of scalding coffee. I smiled, knowing we had been blessed with another beautiful day in which to explore the wilderness together.

The Rocky Mountain chain stretches from the Yukon Territory to Mexico, but it is here in Alberta that the mountain peaks are the most dramatic. The Eastern Slopes region is the province's most distinctive area, the place where the Rockies first rise from the plains. Although most of us would like to believe the Eastern Slopes are still untouched, much of the area has already been greatly changed. Most of this man-made change has occurred rapidly since the early 1950s. In many places, exploration roads, oil and gas wells, pipelines, stripmines and logging operations have left their mark on the land.

The Alberta Wilderness Association believes that the remaining wilderness lands on Alberta's Eastern Slopes should be set aside now from further development. These are the proposed *Wildland Recreation Areas,* those few remaining natural land areas in the Eastern Slopes whose preservation can ensure that Albertans never lose the opportunity to experience and understand nature's frontier – our living heritage. Today, none of these wilderness lands is protected by legislation, even though public hearings and an opinion poll in 1973 found that the majority of Albertans supported proposals for their protection.

An Orientation

In view of the extensive resource development on the Eastern Slopes today, only limited areas remain which qualify for wilderness protection. Eleven of these areas are discussed in this book: Folding Mountain, White Goat, Ram/Whiterabbit, Panther Corners, Burnt Timber, South Ghost, Elbow Sheep, Upper Oldman, North Porcupine Hills, The Whaleback, and

South Castle. Two other areas, the Upper Kananaskis and the Wild Kakwa, are briefly described. The Upper Kananaskis was proposed as a Wildland Recreational Area in 1973 and is now part of a Provincial Park. The Wild Kakwa identified for provincial park designation in 1977 is still under review.

All but one of the proposed areas are located in the high remote headwaters regions of the Eastern Slopes. That's how far back our wild frontier has been pushed. Any delay in protection for these last wild areas may seal their fate – for wilderness, the battle can be lost only once. Because wilderness is a product of centuries of natural processes, we cannot "build" more wilderness. There is no substitute for wilderness. What we now have is all we shall ever have. What is lost today cannot be recovered.

Wildlands are an important link to our past and to our future. The wilderness has shaped our heritage. Our Canadian identity has been molded by the qualities of a wild and powerful land. Today, our wilderness is shrinking rapidly. The wilderness lands we describe in this book are key wild regions which must be preserved for recreation, scientific use, watershed protection, conservation of fish and wildlife, and conservation of our cultural heritage, as well as for their inherent natural beauty.

The Alberta Wilderness Association believes the economic advantages of developing the Eastern Slopes for their resources will be outweighed by the economic advantage of establishing a defined system of wilderness lands for recreation. These slopes lie adjacent to Alberta's main population corridor which stretches from Edmonton to Lethbridge. Now and in the future, city residents and out-of-

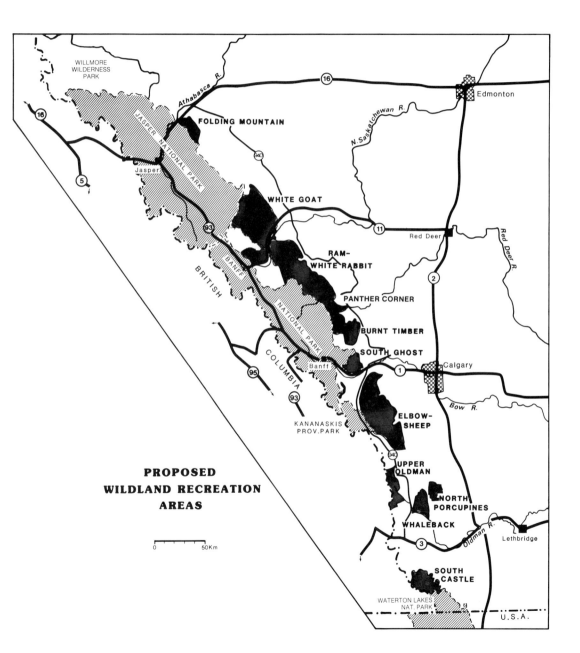

**PROPOSED
WILDLAND RECREATION
AREAS**

province visitors, together with rural Albertans, will seek revitalization in the wild country of the Eastern Slopes.

In the pages that follow, explore the remaining Eastern Slopes wilderness with us. Share our excitement as you read about the personal experiences our members enjoyed while exploring the proposed "Wildland Recreation Areas".

Mountain goat, skilled climber of rocky crags.

Watershed Protection

The high country of the Eastern Slopes has long been considered to have its primary or best use in producing a continuous flow of pure, clean water. The Eastern Rockies Forest Conservation Board was established in 1948 to ensure that the watershed potential of these high elevation lands was not allowed to deteriorate. The water that is gathered on the Eastern Slopes is important not only to Albertans but to residents of Saskatchewan and Manitoba as well. Recognizing that watershed protection is the highest priority use of the Eastern Slopes, establishing Wildland Recreation Areas will help to assure that the quality of this resource never deteriorates.

Climate

The Eastern Slopes are well suited for recreation. Located on the lee or "rain shadow" side of the Continental Divide, precipitation in the east slope mountains and foothills is comparatively low. The Eastern Slopes receive less rain in the summer and have fewer fogged-in and cloudy days than lands to the west. During the winter, snowfall is also less and because of the warm chinook winds, the snowpack disappears relatively soon in the spring, usually opening the areas early in the year for summer recreation. Because of those dry conditions, there is little undergrowth in the Eastern Slopes forests, making them easily accessible.

Vegetation

Generally speaking, up to 1 525 metres elevation the forests of the Eastern Slopes are made up of relatively dense stands of white spruce and a mix of Engelmann spruce and alpine fir, with alpine tundra occurring above treeline. To the casual observer the two spruces are hard to tell apart, with identification made even more difficult by the interbreeding which may occur at middle elevation.

This forest type is the final stage to which the natural forest vegetation on the Eastern Slopes progresses. However, fire plays a key role in the Eastern Slopes forests and is a natural part of these ecosystems.

After a fire, the first evergreen trees to reseed are lodgepole pine, not spruce. The tightly sealed seed cone of this pine can withstand the high temperatures of a forest fire. In the heat of the fire, the lodgepole cones open sooner than they would normally do, allowing the seeds to be shed shortly after the fire onto the open mineral soil. Many of the forests on the Eastern Slopes are fire successional or "seral" lodgepole pine. The pine forests will not remain indefinitely. Eventually, the seedlings of spruce, which are tolerant of the shade of the lodgepole forest, will overtake the pine. Finally, the older pine from 80 to 120 years of age die. Young pines are not produced because of their inability to tolerate the dense shade of the forest. This change in the forest is called "succession", a process which may take up to 300 years from start to finish. Without fire, the spruce stage of forest development is self-sustaining. Younger saplings take the place of older trees as they senesce and succumb to wind, insect attacks or disease. Individual trees will survive to over 400 years of age, while the climax forest, especially at high elevations, may be 500 to 1,000 years old before perishing in the next fire.

A mature spruce forest is dark, cool and moist. Little light passes through to the ground, resulting in sparse, light undergrowth that makes hiking and travel on horseback relatively easy, and very pleasant on a hot summer day. The young lodgepole forest, on the other hand, is often quite dense. The trees may only be separated by inches, and densities of several thousand trees per hectare are common. Passage through these "dog hair" stands is difficult and frustrating. It's best to try and travel around young lodgepole stands. Old pine forests are more open and quite dry, with sparse ground cover. These mature lodgepole stands have thinned themselves, the weaker trees dying from competition. By the time the lodgepole forest reaches maturity, the remaining trees are well spaced and travel is easy.

Depending on their location, a wide assortment of plants can be found on the floor of spruce-pine forests, including ground juniper, wild rose, horsetail, forget-me-not, buffalo-berry, huckleberry, cinquefoil, twin-flower, grouseberry, heart-leaved arnica, globe-flower, one-flowered Clintonia, one-flowered and pink wintergreen, bunchberry and bearberry. In moist, completely shaded areas, thick feather moss carpets the forest floor.

At lower elevations, the spruce-pine forest may also include the Douglas fir, a tree common to the west of the Rocky Mountains. In Alberta, this tree is found most often on the southwest-facing slopes in areas where the climate is dominated by chinooks. In the North Porcupine Hills and Whaleback, the forests have a sizable component of Douglas fir. Balsam poplar and aspen poplar, interspersed with meadows and willow shrublands, usually inhabit the valley floors. At high elevation, the broad band of Engelmann spruce and alpine fir forests extending to timberline is referred to as the subalpine. The timberline fluctuates around the 2000 metre elevation in the southern Rockies to 1500 metres in the northern Rockies. Above timberline, the forest gives way to small clumps of dwarfed trees interspersed with meadow. In addition to Engelmann spruce and alpine fir, white-bark pine and limber pine occur along ridgelines, and alpine larch grow on more sheltered slopes. The larch is an interesting conifer which loses its needles each fall. Just prior to dropping, the needles turn from green to a spectacular golden colour, adding a brilliant hue to the autumn mountains. Each spring, soft light green new needles reappear.

Gnarled and dwarf tree colonies known as Krummholz or elfinwood are common at treeline. A tree only one metre in height may be 200 to 300 years old. Snow, cold temperatures, a very short growing season and high winds drastically affect plant growth here. Associated with the dwarf alpine fir and gnarled limber and lodgepole pine are crowberry, purple, yellow and white mountain heathers, numerous grasses, the glacier lily, western anemone, and wild chives.

The high alpine tundra situated above the treeline is completely devoid of trees. This is impressive hiking country, offering extensive and often spectacular views, but it is also the most fragile of the vegetation areas. If conditions are right, especially near streamlets or glacier and snow melts, lush flower meadows may be found. Most of the plants of the subalpine will be found here in a dwarf form along with other flowers such as alpine harebell, Lyall's ironplant, rock-jasmine, Jacob's-ladder, purple saxifrage, moss campion, alpine bearberry, snow willow, alpine poppy and alpine cinquefoil. Hundreds of species of flowering plants await the interested amateur or professional botanist.

Some high alpine slopes will be almost barren, having little plant growth on the gravelly soil. As well, much of the Eastern Slopes extend beyond the alpine tundra into bare rock and snow, and the dramatic peaks of the Rockies themselves.

Wildlife

The proposed Wildland Recreation Areas, together with the adjacent Rocky Mountain National Parks and Alberta's four established Wilderness Areas, present the best opportunity in North America for protecting in perpetuity the wildlife associated with the Rocky Mountains. Rocky Mountain wildlife, of which the large mammals have been made world-renowned through art, photography, hunting and sightseeing excursions, is a precious part of the national heritage of not only Albertans but of citizens of the world.

It was to ensure the protection and continued existence of this invaluable heritage that the four Rocky Mountain National Parks – Banff, Jasper, Yoho and Kootenay – were declared a World Heritage Site, and Waterton Lakes National Park

ABOVE: *Rocky mountain bighorn sheep on the move.* RIGHT: *Bluegrouse can be found on high timbered ridges and mountain slopes throughout the Eastern Slopes.* FAR RIGHT: *A mule deer will risk being seen in order to keep potential enemies under observation.*

was made an International Biosphere Reserve. Several populations of large mammals found inside these sites, like the elk or grizzly, are equally dependent on adjacent lands, many of which lie within the proposed Wildland Recreation Areas.

Often overlooked by past wildlife management, non-game species such as song birds are increasingly important to the general public, providing immeasurable hours of wildlife viewing pleasure. Birds such as cavity nesters and raptors, along with many of the furbearing animals which are the cornerstone of the fur industry, depend on old growth forest. The proposed Wildland Recreation Areas would provide protection for these dynamic old growth forests and their wild inhabitants.

On Alberta's Eastern Slopes all of the North American big game animals except antelope can be found. Mountain goat, Rocky Mountain bighorn sheep, elk and moose, as well as woodland caribou in the northern segment, are all present. The less accessible regions retain populations of grizzly, cougar and wolf. Black bear are common throughout. Generally the proposed Wildland Recreation Areas encompass much of the higher quality wildlife ranges and many of the critical winter habitats on the Eastern Slopes.

Mule deer are widely distributed and in recent years the white-tailed deer has become increasingly common in the foothills and major drainages of the front ranges. At high elevations, however, neither mule deer nor white-tail deer become abundant because of the severe snow conditions and limited winter ranges. Both deer species are localized in winter on key ranges where food and shelter are both available. In summer, when conditions are more favourable, populations are widely distributed, although their numbers may be sparse. Deer depend heavily on winter range, and loss of a key winter range, for instance to stripmining, will decimate the population. Deer require deciduous forest of aspen poplar, which is usually found on the lower slopes and in the valleys and on south-facing hillsides of major drainages.

The behavior patterns of white-tail and mule deer differ considerably. Mule deer prefer a more open habitat than do white-tail and thus commonly winter at higher elevations. As a result, the mule deer range farther west on the Eastern Slopes than the white-tail. Mule deer are more inclined to run from their enemies, while the white-tail will often either stand and let a predator walk right by, or will sneak away to escape danger. A white-tail, standing in a freeze position, is one of the most difficult animals to observe. The mule deer, on the other hand, likes to see its enemy and will risk being seen to gain this advantage. Places like Trout Creek in the North Porcupines are ideal mule deer country, being relatively open with plenty of aspen and wet enough for good shrub stands.

The Rocky Mountain bighorn sheep is abundant along the Eastern Slopes, and to most Albertans is synonymous with the Rocky Mountains. The male bighorn is an impressive animal, growing a massive pair of curled horns. The older the animal the greater the curl. Occasionally, very old rams may exhibit horns which spiral around some distance beyond a full circle. The ewes, by comparison, grow only small curved spikes. The horns of the rams are important in the fall during the rut or mating season. Two mature rams will fight one another for the privilege of acquiring a ewe. The rams charge head first, often battering away at each other for hours.

The bighorn is associated with stable, open alpine and subalpine grasslands, and its continued existence depends on whether or not these areas are disturbed. A highly habitual animal which uses long standing traditional ranges, it seldom uses the temporary grasslands which occur after forest fires. The seasonal ranges of the bighorn sheep are usually learned by the young from older members of the population. Unlike moose, few animals wander from these "traditional" ranges. Therefore, re-establishment of populations in areas which had previously been occupied by sheep is difficult. It is imperative that the present winter ranges of bighorn sheep along the Eastern Slopes be retained and treated with care.

The bighorn doesn't migrate from high to low elevations as much as deer or elk. Often it will stay on higher slopes throughout the year. Windblown southwest-facing slopes, which are generally clear of snow, are used as winter range. Lambing takes place in the spring in high secluded areas when the ewes are separated from the rams. The young are often born in precipitous terrain where it would be difficult for a predator to attack the newborn.

Moose are the largest members of the deer family, often growing to four metres in height, half of which is in their long legs. The males display spreading palm-antlers which are grown annually in the late spring or early summer and dropped around the beginning of the next January. Females are antlerless. Unlike the bighorn, the moose has evolved in association with several temporary vegetation types which occur primarily after forest fires. As a result of being dependent on the willow vegetation of burned-over areas, natural populations have fluctuated widely in the past.

One major reason why moose are not as common in the mountains of the south today as they were in the recent past is attributable to the policy of forest fire suppression. The result of this policy has been a tremendous reduction in the number of wildfires, which create willow-browsing areas. As the willow dies out and conifers take over, moose habitat declines. If complete fire suppression continues, soon the only moose ranges will be those small areas of open wet land in valley bottoms or on muskeg flats. The loss of habitat that has resulted from the infrequency of fire, when combined with increased vehicle access and heavier hunting pressure, presents a considerable threat to maintaining a large moose population in the southern part of the Eastern Slopes.

The elk, or wapiti, is truly one of our most magnificent animals. Its graceful curving antlers are perhaps the most spectacular of any North American ungulate. As with the moose and deer, only the males grow antlers. During the mating season, the bull elk grapple with one another, using their antlers as fearsome weapons. During the rut, their bugle, an eerie whistling sound, can often be heard over a distance of several kilometres in the crisp fall air. On rare occasions, the antlers of two elk interlock, and the animals have been known to starve to death.

RIGHT: *The powerful grizzly bear, monarch of the wilderness, can still be found in more remote regions of the Eastern Slopes.*

Elk are grazers and require grasslands as part of their winter and summer range. Like the bighorn, their habitat, especially the limiting winter ranges, needs to be protected from disturbance. Large expanses of wilderness ensure such protection. Most of the proposed Wildland Recreation Areas would act as "wildlife reservoirs" to ensure the maintenance of sizable elk herds. Elk calve and spend their summers in the high elevation meadows, depending on adjacent forests for secure shelter. In fall they migrate eastward to lower, southwest-facing slopes blown free of winter snows.

Elk populations on the Eastern Slopes are much more numerous, particularly in the south, than they were at the turn of the century. A series of very hot and extensive fires along the front ranges cleared vast areas of forested land, producing grasslands ideal for the elk. However, as these areas are invaded by aspen and brush or are re-established in coniferous forest, and as the suppression of fires continues, the ranges are shrinking, and so too will the elk population.

Woodland caribou are the most sensitive of the ungulates to human activity. Far too little is known about their habitat requirements and migration routes in Alberta. The sight of their large gracefully spreading antlers floating across the open expanses of subalpine meadows is now rare in Alberta. In recent years, caribou numbers have plummeted. Dependent on old growth forests, the protection provided by the northern Wildland Recreation Areas in conjunction with the adjacent national park lands may prove essential to their survival.

Mountain goats are not really goats but actually a type of chamois. They spend much of their time on the rocky crags of high ridges. The visitor who only journeys the highway is unlikely to see them. Even a hiker, unless he travels high and knows where to look, may only see goats at a distance, a series of white dots on a rocky ridge. Goats are very sure-footed, moving easily on steep slopes and bluffs. Here the goat is generally safe, for few predators care to come after even the vulnerable young on such difficult terrain. The mountain goat, with its intricate social life and its preference for staying on its home ranges, is very susceptible to decimation by hunting carried out under the standard guidelines used for other ungulates. Lack of knowledge in early game management led to a sharp decline. Hunting closures were invoked for most of the Eastern Slopes, and under more enlightened management these inhabitants of the mountain crags are returning.

Two species of bear exist on the Eastern Slopes. The black bear is present throughout the area. The grizzly, however, is less often seen, having been driven back into the remaining wilderness by the guns, traps and bounties that came with the settlers. The rapid decline in their last wilderness hideouts in Alberta, as well as everywhere else in North America, has resulted in a much reduced grizzly population.

Bears and wolves often present a fearsome prospect to those who have not had the chance to learn about them or do much travelling in the backcountry. Wolves, grizzly and black bears once lived throughout North America, but grizzlies and wolves particularly were so feared by settlers that they were eliminated from all but the more remote areas. An area cannot be counted as wilderness if there are no bears, nor any chance to hear a wolf howl. Bears and wolves are now extinct or protected as endangered species in other lands. Alberta is very fortunate to still have such animals within her boundaries. Much of the wilderness land described in this book remains as excellent wild habitat, essential for the survival of wilderness-dependent species.

Grizzly and black bears have similar diets and habits, although the grizzly is generally found in more open areas and the black bear is more common in forested areas. Grizzlies obtain much of their food, such as their staple of hedysarum roots, by digging with their long front claws. Their love of fall berries and their preference for digging in loose ground are reasons why they are usually seen on avalanche slopes or open hillsides. Black bears rarely dig for food, preferring to "graze" and eat berries in the fall. Grizzlies, like black bears, eat green vegetation and berries, but also eat roots, corms, bulbs and ground squirrels. Both feed on carrion and both are proficient hunters of vulnerable prey such as rodents or young elk and mountain sheep. However, their diet is 90 percent vegetation.

Perhaps the small mammals, particularly rabbits and rodents such as the well known ground squirrel, have suffered least from man's activities. They are still abundant and are an important part of the diet of almost all the predators of the Eastern Slopes, especially the coyote. Ground squirrel colonies are particularly numerous on the same open slopes that are favoured by species such as elk and bighorn sheep. Pikas and hoary marmots occupy high alpine rock slides and burrow sites, telling of their presence by sharp squeals, in the case of the pika, or shrill whistles in the case of the marmot. Their warning sounds are synonymous with alpine wilderness.

The cougar is king of the quiet wilderness.

The cougar, variously known in different regions as the panther, puma, or mountain lion.

Once he inhabited virtually all of North America, but today is confined to the remnants of the true wilderness and is rarely seen. Nevertheless, cougars maintain healthy populations in the proposed Whaleback, Elbow/ Sheep and North Porcupine Hills Wildland Recreation Areas where they feed freely on deer, elk, moose and smaller animals like porcupines.

The wolverine, another wilderness – dependent carnivore, has become rare in the province, largely due to the decline in the amount of old growth forest where it generally makes its home.

Cougar, grizzly and wolf play a role in the natural dynamics of ungulate populations. All of these predators have been decimated by man, and continuing loss of secure habitat is a major threat to stable populations. However, in Alberta all have acquired some degree of protection thanks to careful controls on hunting and trapping.

History

For centuries before the Canadian Pacific Railway's first transcontinental passenger train chugged through western Canada in the 1880s, the Eastern Slopes were used mostly by Indians for hunting grounds. Explorers and fur traders who made inroads into and through the Rocky Mountains in the late 1700s and early 1800s were the first to map the Eastern Slopes and introduce the Rocky Mountains to the outside world. The CPR transcontinental heralded a new era for the fledgling city of Calgary and its pride, the nearby Rocky Mountains. The railroad brought hunters, modern explorers and sightseers to the scenic wonders and playgrounds of Alberta's Eastern Slopes. One could not have imagined that such vast and impervious wilderness could ever be influenced by man. But by the early 1900s demands upon the Eastern Slopes were mounting and the Dominion government took measures to manage the Eastern Slopes timber and water resources. The Forest Reserves Act was introduced to prohibit settlement for all but backcountry loggers and miners. In 1911, Parliament established the Rocky Mountains National Forest, dedicated to the perpetuation of timber and watersheds. As described by a 1927 government brochure:

> These forests are areas of non-agricultural lands, established primarily for the protection and reproduction of timber, for the protection of watershed, and for the maintenance of conditions favourable to a continous water supply and for the protection of animals, birds and fish.

The brochure went on to emphasize the increasing importance of aesthetics and recreation:

> The scenic and recreational values of these forests are now deemed to be resources of major importance … the part played by our National Forests is daily becoming a more important factor in the economic wealth, health and happiness of our country.

Recreation in the Eastern Slopes, particularly those areas adjacent to Calgary and southern communities, is not some new concept that has emerged only within the last decade. At first there were a few aristocrats, such as the Earl of Southesk, who took an 1859 hunting excursion along the eastern boundary of present-day Jasper National Park. By 1927, government brochures on the Bow River National Forest were reporting, "The number of people in this country who go into the forest on picnic, camping, fishing or hunting trips is increasing year to year by leaps and bounds."

The national park system begun in 1885 around the Banff Hot Springs expanded to include lands in the presently proposed Wildland Recreation Areas. In 1911, all the Alberta Rocky Mountain National Parks were severely cut back in size.

The railways, which were committed to making the national parks into tourist meccas, the Campfire Club of America, and the Alberta Fish and Game Protection Association, concerned about the effect such a reduction in parkland would have on wildlife, set up a storm of protest. By 1917, the parks were again enlarged, only to be once more reduced during 1920-1930 to their present-day boundaries.

In the early 1930s, ownership of Eastern Slopes resources was transferred from the federal to the provincial government. The Alberta government much later took some steps to protect Alberta's outstanding wilderness lands, but stopped far short of the public's expectations. In 1959, Willmore Wilderness Park on the northern boundary of Jasper Park was established. To this day, the Act establishing this park does not protect it from reduction in size, motorized use, or resource development. Reduced twice by a total of 969 square kilometres and periodically threatened by development, today's 4598 square kilometre Willmore Wilderness Park is maintained intact by the constant vigilance of the Alberta public. In 1971, the 443 square kilometre White Goat, 412 square kilometre Siffleur and 152 square kilometre Ghost River Wilderness Areas were created through Alberta's new Wilderness Areas Act. This legislation, unlike other North American wilderness legislation, does not permit many of the traditional forms of wilderness recreation like fishing, hunting or horseback riding. Through influence of politicians who at the time believed wilderness areas should be no larger than what can be walked across in a day, (approximately 20 kilometres by 20 kilometres), two-thirds of the original White Goat Wilderness Park was withdrawn from protection when the area was placed under the 1971 Wilderness Areas Act.

Extraction of minerals and hydrocarbons intensified in the 1940s through to the late 1960s. The public began protesting the impending exploitation of their Eastern Slopes. In 1973, the new provincial Conservative government placed a moratorium on further development in the Eastern Slopes. A series of public hearings were held by the Environment Conservation Authority (the ECA), and an opinion poll was taken.

After nearly a year of public hearings, the ECA released its findings in 1974. The ECA found that 90 percent of the Albertans surveyed "favored preservation of nature and restoration of areas which have suffered environmental degradation. The large majority of Albertans best enjoy the Eastern Slopes for their scenic qualities and the opportunity to communicate with nature in its unspoiled state."

During the public hearings, the Alberta Wilderness Association submitted its recommendations for the establishment of Wildland Recreation Areas in the province's Eastern Slopes. The Wild Kakwa Society submitted a similar proposal for the Kakwa River drainage on the north side of Willmore Wilderness Park. These proposals for areas "where most outdoor activities including hunting are allowed, but where motorized vehicles and natural resource industries are forbidden" won broad support from a variety of interests, from private citizens to city councils and chambers of commerce. The majority of Albertans polled indicated they supported the establishment of such areas.

The ECA's follow-up report on the public hearings recommended the establishment of Wildland Recreation Areas and indicated that a clear majority of Albertans agreed.

With the findings of the ECA known, an inventory and assessment of Eastern Slopes lands was conducted and various zones were identified according to their potential for resource extraction, timber, tourism, recreation and wildlife.

In 1975, the Minister of the Environment, commenting on the 1974 recommendations of the ECA, stated:

> Their fifth recommendation [states that] certain lands should be reserved for a limited use or a limited combination of uses such as wildland recreation areas, provincial parks and wilderness areas. More sensitive areas should be protected by limited access and I think I can say that we have accepted that recommendation 100% and I expect during the next couple of years to see various pieces of legislation and regulations introduced that will bring protection to and definition of these kinds of areas.

A moratorium on all development was continued through to 1977 for the proposed Wildland Recreation Areas. The Policy for Resource Management of the Eastern Slopes was released by the government in 1977. Albertans were informed that there would be no legislation to protect Wildland Recreation Areas; instead the protection of these lands would be taken care of through the Prime Protection Zoning of the new Policy. None of the protective designations the Environment Minister spoke of in 1975 have come about, with the exception of one provincial park.

The Alberta Coal Policy of 1976 complemented the Eastern Slopes Policy by providing a similar approach to managing coal exploration and development. Most critical wildlife habitat and mountain landscapes, for instance, would be in Category I of the Coal Policy, by which exploration or development of coal resources would be forbidden and existing leases bought back or allowed to lapse without development.

The Prime Protection Zoning provided in the Eastern Slopes Policy as well as in Category I of the Coal Policy provides protection in theory for key Eastern Slopes areas, but still lacks legislation to enforce its good intentions. These are policies, not legislation, and thus can easily be altered by Cabinet or individual ministers. Even in the Prime Protection areas recognized in the Policy as deserving of utmost protection, step-out drilling and recreation development may occur. In effect, motorized use throughout the Prime Protection Zone lands is permitted. Since 1985, legislation to control motorized use has been in effect for only two percent of these Prime Protection Zone lands.

In 1984, the provincial government unilaterally changed the Eastern Slopes Policy. Revisions shifted the policy's focus from conservation and protection of the Eastern Slopes to development. Now more than ever

Alberta's few remaining wilderness lands are threatened.

On April 4, 1986, the Alberta government announced the naming of the Bighorn Wildland Recreation Area which encompasses the Association's proposed White Goat, Ram/ Whiterabbit and Panther Corners Wildland Recreation Areas. As the 1984 Eastern Slopes Policy still applies to this area, it remains to be seen if the Bighorn Wildland Recreation Area will be afforded legal protection.

The Alberta Wilderness Association's "Wildlands for Recreation" proposals today include 11 wilderness areas along the Eastern Slopes. These lands, totalling 6460 square kilometres or seven percent of the Eastern Slopes, require protection by law from activities which detract from their wilderness qualities and inherent recreation and tourism value.

Each proposed Wildland Recreation Area was selected for a number of reasons:

- A natural or primitive character largely unaffected by man, or the ability to be reclaimed to this state within a relatively short time.

- The potential for primitive, non-motorized, and unconfined wilderness recreation, with opportunities for solitude.

- Sufficient size to make practical the protection of its vegetation and wildlife and its use for extended trips.

- The presence of representative or unique ecological features such as vegetation, land forms or wildlife.

- Scenic qualities.

- **Good accessibility from populated urban areas.**

- Historical or archaeological importance.

- Opportunities for nature appreciation and understanding.

- Scientific value.

All of the proposed Wildland Recreation Areas are on publicly owned land, held in trust for Albertans by the Alberta Forest Service.

Some of the proposed Wildland Recreation Areas are recovering from past abuses. Some are threatened by current or future industrial intrusions. Others have no apparent commercial resource development value, so that their wilderness lands can be relatively easily protected. The proposed Wildland Recreation Areas include representations of all Rocky Mountain and foothills ecosystems, as well as aspects of our cultural heritage.

When selecting the proposed Wildland Recreation Areas, the technical advisors carefully considered existing or potential resource uses. Those selected are believed to have their greatest potential as recreational wilderness areas, and in total add up to about seven percent of the 92 000 square kilometres that comprise the Eastern Slopes. To balance the wilderness and user aspects of Wildland Recreation Areas, and to ensure that the benefits of their untrammelled state are available for future generations, protection of these areas must be enforced by legislation.

Wild Kakwa
Alpland of a Thousand Wonders

Lying on the northern boundary of Willmore Wilderness Park where the provincial border swings north away from the northwest-trending Continental Divide, the Kakwa is a Rocky Mountain wilderness described by those who have seen it as an "alpland of a thousand wonders." The provincial boundary which separates the Alberta portion from the British Columbia side of the Wild Kakwa is an impossible one to draw in reality. The wilderness is indifferent to man-made boundaries.

Between the mountains in the southwest of the Alberta Kakwa and the more softly rounded foothills of the northern and eastern portions lie narrow forested valleys and a high alpine plateau. This area is the scenic doorstep to the headwaters of the Kakwa and McGregor rivers, the Kakwa, Babette and Cecilia lakes and the towering massif of Mount Sir Alexander just over the provincial border in British Columbia. There to meet the visitor are wilderness scenes of crystal lakes at the foot of glacier-capped peaks, untrammelled scenes equal to those which awed Tom Wilson in 1882, the first white man to see the now-world-renowned Lake Louise.

At the time of writing this book, it is hoped that formal legislated protection is well on its way for the Wild Kakwa in Alberta.

In 1973, the Wild Kakwa Society, "dedicated to saving wilderness in the Peace," first proposed protection for the Wild Kakwa under the Wilderness Areas Act. This 477 square kilometre area is also considered part of an Interprovincial Tri-Park Proposal which has been in existence for over a decade. The proposal consists of the Wild Kakwa of Alberta, Willmore Wilderness Park and the Kakwa/Mount Sir Alexander area of British Columbia.

In 1974, the Alberta government announced plans to establish a large provincial park to protect the Kakwa and South Kakwa rivers. Following this, in 1977, the Alberta government approached the British Columbia government hoping to establish the Interprovincial Tri-Park.

However, at that time, as now, the British Columbia government was not prepared to move on park status for the area.

Even though it appeared on the Alberta road maps as a provincial park, the Wild Kakwa since 1970 has alternated in its management between the Alberta Forest Service and Alberta Parks, currently resting in the hands of the Alberta Forest Service. Since its transfer back to the Forest Service, the Wild Kakwa has been managed along the same lines as Willmore Wilderness Park, though the government has been reluctant to include it under the protection of the Willmore Wilderness Park Act. Motorized use inside the area is now prohibited by Forest Land Use Zone legislation. It remains department policy not to approve any recreation or resource developments within the Wild Kakwa.

For those wanting to visit this wilderness, access can be gained by a gravel road from Grande Prairie which leads to within two kilometres of the Kakwa Falls, or by horse or foot from Willmore Wilderness Park.

Protection of the entire Alberta/British Columbia Kakwa would preserve for Canadians a unique piece of their cultural and natural heritage: the chance to experience the challenges and sense of discovery which met those first guides and tourists who saw today's famed areas such as Lake Louise before they evolved into commercial tourist areas.

RIGHT: *The high alpine plateau of the Wild Kakwa as seen in the vicinity of Bank Creek.*

Folding Mountain
A Pocket Wilderness

They took horses up there!? I was standing on a faded old trail in the shade of the last trees looking up at a steep scree slope, the top etched against the sky in shale rock. The "Stone Steps", Jim Redmond had called them in his description of "Charlie's Pass". But seeing the view right there in front of me, my mind questioned if I'd found the right trail at all!

This route into the "pocket wilderness" area of Folding Mountain has an obscure beginning on the south side of the Yellowhead Highway. However, shortly upon joining the main trail out of the old Circle M Ranch, it turned into one of those charming, logically located old outfitting trails winding its way southeast up along a ridge to Folding Mountain. Passing across open west-facing meadows on the ridge, one would be a fool not to take a break from the steady climb to contemplate the outstanding scenery.

It's a view that takes one up the Athabasca River valley into present-day Jasper National Park, and back into the history of the Canadian Rockies. Indians, mountain men, fur traders and railway men madly laying two separate lines of steel in the bid to be the first through Yellowhead Pass had all, in their own time, pitted their

RIGHT: *The exquisitely delicate sparrow's egg orchid.*

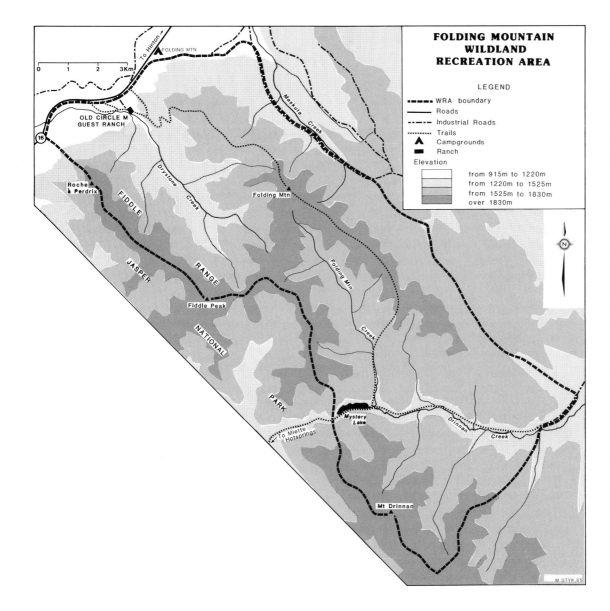

survival skills against the Athabasca's treacherous route through the stone wall of the Rockies. Today, a broad ribbon of pavement and one railroad carries travellers safely past Disaster Point on their way into Jasper. Most travellers are probably unaware of the past hardships of their route, and likely no one was aware of my solitary viewpoint in the Wildland on the edge of the park.

I had been into the area of the proposed Folding Mountain Wildland before via a different route from the south, starting at Miette Hot Springs in Jasper Park. Travelling a trail older than the park itself, the Miette route was followed by the early residents of the Luscar coal fields to the east on their regular treks to the soothing waters of the hot springs. Now the trail carries a steady flow of people in the opposite direction. Most of them carry the tell-tale fishing rod, bound for Mystery Lake. You might almost swear you had somehow arrived on the British Columbia side of the Continental Divide upon reaching Mystery Lake. It's a small deep lake encircled by a characteristic steep rocky shore. Surrounding the lake is a thick dark forest edged with a lush growth of cow parsnip, valerian and tall larkspur. Maybe it was the steady drizzle that day that completed the British Columbia mirage.

But I was told that I had stopped short of finding the heart and soul of this area – the heart that made the protection of this small 109 square kilometre wildland the focus of entire lifetimes. To know the Wildland, my guides had told me, I must also see Folding Mountain itself. So, with my daypack weighted down with two cameras, assorted lenses, filters and floral identification books, I continued to plod up the loose scree slope to find what had left the naturalists who had seen this area so short of words to describe it.

It was only through the efforts of Charlie and Mona Matheson that the "trail" before me was there at all. When they retired from the Park Warden Service and started the Circle M Ranch in 1940, Charlie set to work blazing the trail over the 2188 metre peak of Folding Mountain to Mystery Lake. Undaunted by the impassible rock slide on the north side of the peak, he enlisted the help of Frank and David Moberly, descendents of the first guide and entrepreneur to settle in the region, to clear this wild passage.

I had seen quite an array of our native orchids along the route below: the Franklin's or sparrow's-egg orchid, the brilliant calypso orchid, and the yellow lady's-slipper which flower pickers have exterminated from several other areas. However, claims that almost every wild flower in R.G.H. Cormack's *Wild Flowers of Alberta* could be found in this small area, a relatively short walk from a major highway, still seemed rather exaggerated.

I plodded on further; a few more steps would bring me in view of the unknown, the other side of Folding Mountain. However, unable to pass up a good photo, I snapped some shots of a rich yellow clump of alpine cinquefoil held by craggy black shale up against the sky.

The view at the end of those few steps

laid all charges of exaggeration to rest. An alpine meadow intricately woven with countless blossoms spread before me to the west amongst the stark peaks of the Fiddle Range. The daypack with its forgotten floral keys was dropped on the alpine tundra and unmarked time was spent savouring each splash of colour. Flowers – the earth's laughter. Pikas scrambled and squealed at the strange creature sprawled out in numerous prone positions with camera in hand. But then, such loveliness deserves more than just pictures. The books were dug out and more time was idled away in this well stocked botanical garden, putting names to the splashes of colour. White camas, moss campion, stonecrop, mountain avens, alpine harebells, alpine bearberry, Lyall's ironplant, townsendia, various saxifrages and heather - the list rambled on with the day.

Eager to take more photos as the sinking sun spread a golden hue over the landscape, I almost overstayed my time. It was a quick trip back. I scrambled down the scree, and strode with new energy through the alpine fir and Engelmann spruce, across the open grass meadows and finally out of the lodgepole pine forest at the highway.

Flinging my daypack into my truck as the traffic whizzed by, I recalled how the Moberlys, the Mathesons, Bill Switzer and finally Jim Redmond had spoken and written about protecting such wilderness "so that without great expense our children may backpack into a very wild natural area with a real challenge." They're all gone now and I'm left with but one way to thank them for my day on Folding Mountain and the

treasures my camera did and didn't take – to work as they did to make sure this place is here for our children.

The smallest of the proposed Wildlands for Recreation, Folding Mountain is not to be underestimated because of its size. In its 109 square kilometres (an area less than one-quarter the size of Edmonton) dense forests, grassy slopes and alpine meadows harbor more than 200 species of Rocky Mountain wildflowers.

Folding Mountain reveals the drama of the earth's forces that created it. This massive faulted, folded and twisted rock rises like a gateway sentinel on the south edge of the Yellowhead Highway near the east entrance of Jasper National Park. This small wilderness lies between the foothills and the mountains. Roche à Perdrix, which forms the western boundary of the wilderness, is the beginning of the front ranges of the Rockies.

The Yellowhead Route along the wide Athabasca River valley was regularly navigated by Indian peoples who hunted and gathered in the region as early as 12,000 years ago. In 1811, looking for a pass rumoured to be used by Nipissing Indians and trappers, David Thompson followed this route to the Athabasca Pass. Thompson was forced into his explorations which lead to this discovery because the Peigans, fearing the whites would trade guns to the Kootenay

Indians, had closed the Howse Pass further south on the Saskatchewan River.

Once part of Jasper National Park, Folding Mountain today shares the park's eastern border. This small wilderness's brief inclusion in the national park along with its possibilities as a provincial park deferred exploration and development of its resources. The area was a favourite of the late Bill Switzer, a former MLA for Edson between 1965 and 1969. Sadly, his dream to establish a wilderness park in the area was unfulfilled and instead a small provincial park, William Switzer Memorial Park, was established north of Hinton on the Grande Cache Highway.

The proposed Folding Mountain Wildland Recreation Area, though small, remains a truly wild area which offers solitude to those desiring a short wilderness trip with one to three days of nature appreciation or fishing.

Geological History

The Folding Mountain area marks the interface between the foothills and the front ranges of the Rocky Mountains. As the name suggests, the area was crumpled and distorted by the earth's mountain-building forces. These disturbances, beginning perhaps 70 million years ago, caused deeply buried Paleozoic limestones and calcareous shale to be pushed to the surface along enormous thrust faults. Many of these rocks are over 500 million years old.

Major river valleys, such as the Athabasca, had been eroded by water long before the ice ages began. During the ice ages, these were filled with glacial ice originating in the mountains. The present landscape was shaped by these moving ice masses, which ground their way eastwards to merge with the ice sheets advancing across Alberta from the north. When the ice receded some 10,000 years ago, the rivers resumed their courses, providing corridors for the movement of wildlife and people.

Human History

The Folding Mountain wilderness has been home to Indian peoples for many years. The Sarcee Indians are believed to have inhabited lands east of the main ranges of the Rocky Mountains, including the Folding Mountain area. Moving over the years from northern Alberta, the Sarcees travelled slowly southward, eventually halting at their current location near Calgary. As the fur trade gained momentum, some Indians of eastern Canada such as the Cree, Ojibwa, Iroquois and Algonquin moved west to work for fur trading companies. Many of these people settled along the Yellowhead Route from today's Hinton region, which includes Folding Mountain, west to the headwaters of the Fraser River. Early white fur traders and explorers often commented on the number and variety of Indian peoples in this region.

The Yellowhead Trail was a major travel route for passage either on foot or by horse from early native days up until the early 1900s. The route followed the south shore of the Athabasca and kept to high land along the north-facing slopes of the Folding Mountain Wildland. This high elevation trail avoided the muskeg of the Athabasca Valley until 12 kilometres further southwest, where the steep slippery rock of Disaster Point had to be ascended to avoid the deadly waters of the Athabasca.

Following the Yellowhead Route, David Thompson and his entourage of 24 men and 24 horses reached Brule Lake just north of the proposed Wildland Recreation Area on December 3, 1810. The party camped near the lake for nearly a month, building snowshoes and sleds and storing food in preparation for the rigorous journey across the mountains. On January 10, 1811, Thompson crossed the summit of the Continental Divide, discovering the Athabasca Pass and the existence of what would later become a major east-west trading corridor across the Rockies.

David Thompson was the first white man to travel through and map this area. Parts of his maps were still included in the government maps as late as 1916.

Other early visitors to the Folding Mountain area include artist Paul Kane, Jesuit missionary Father Pierre Jean De Smet and Palliser's geologist, Dr. James Hector. The Overlanders of 1862, a group of 115 eastern fortune seekers en route to the gold hills of the Caribou, camped at the foot of the Rockies near or possibly in the proposed Wildland Recreation Area. A short distance west along the Yellowhead Route, they encountered terrible muskeg and rugged terrain as well as a scarcity of food. Finally they learned the truth about their dream: there was no gold.

In the late 1800s, the Dominion government was surveying passes across the Continental Divide to determine their feasibility as transcontinental railroad routes to link the new province of British Columbia with the railways of the east. All reports indicated the Yellowhead Route to be the best; however, the government decided on Kicking Horse Pass because it was further south and thus more likely to secure territory eyed by the Americans. Then, in 1911, both the Canadian Northern and the Grand Trunk Pacific railways laid track past Folding Mountain in a race to be the first line through the Yellowhead Pass. The demand for steel with the outbreak of the First World War put an end to the race. One track was kept along the best grades, with the abandoned grade eventually becoming the bed for today's Yellowhead Highway.

Even before Jasper National Park became a park, people from the Coal Branch at Luscar could follow a trail up Drinnan Creek to Mystery Lake and west to Miette Hot Springs. In 1907, "Jasper Forest Park" was established as a scenic right-of-way to lure tourists who would be arriving on the railroad. At that time, the park encompassed about 11 400 square kilometres of land, including Folding Mountain. One of the national park trails developed to patrol the area skirted around the eastern side of Folding Mountain, and a backcountry patrol cabin was constructed along that trail. That

original trail and government axe-blazed trees were still intact in 1963 (the valley and lower slopes on the eastern side of Folding Mountain have since been logged, obliterating the trail). By that time Jasper Park had been reduced by two boundary changes to its present size of 10 878 square kilometres, with the Folding Mountain area lying just outside its protective boundary.

Facilities were developed to accommodate the tourists, hunters and modern explorers that the new railroad brought to the region. In 1940, retired Jasper Park warden Charles Matheson and his wife Mona established the Circle M guest ranch at Drystone Creek on the northern border of the proposed Wildland Recreation Area. Matheson blazed and maintained riding trails in this wilderness area until they sold the ranch 13 years later. Part of Matheson's hard work included the construction of a shorter and more scenic trail from his ranch to Mystery Lake. Unlike the earlier park service trail, the Matheson Trail was constructed over the top of Folding Mountain.

It wasn't until 1963, following a second change of hands, that guest use of the trails was resumed by the Circle M. Jim and Kay Redmond operated the business until fairly recently, outfitting and guiding an international clientele into the backcountry of Folding Mountain. Visitors were also occasionally guided into eastern and northern sections of Jasper Park and as far north as Willmore Wilderness Park. It was the Redmonds who first brought concerns for protecting the Folding Mountain area to the attention of the Alberta Wilderness Association and the public.

Wildlife and Vegetation

The Folding Mountain landscape is one of low lying balsam and aspen poplar, leading to dense Engelmann spruce and alpine fir at tree line and opening into sweeping alpine meadows above 1850 metres elevation. Centred around the rocky mass of Folding Mountain, this pocket wilderness is a natural botanical garden with a full array of Rocky Mountain plants. Though far too small to encompass the home range of most larger animals, the area is used by a variety of mountain wildlife, and is critical winter habitat for some.

Like most mountain regions, vegetation and wildlife communities in the Folding Mountain wilderness change with elevation and the direction that the slopes face. Moose are sometimes seen lumbering through low-lying areas where balsam and aspen poplar are abundant and where black spruce, willow and green alder thickets cluster in wet areas. Bighorn sheep feed on the dry south-facing slopes where forest cover gives way to wheat grass and shrubby plants such as bearberry, buffalo-berry and juniper. A band of one hundred bighorn sheep lives along the park boundary portion of this wilderness area. The entire Folding Mountain area provides critical winter range for these bighorn sheep.

The lower mountain slopes are forested with lodgepole pine and white spruce. These are generally replaced by Engelmann spruce and alpine fir at higher elevations. As the tree cover disperses at about 1850 metres, typical alpine tundra of dwarf shrubs, mosses, lichens and a carpet of wildflowers predominates.

The top and sides of Folding Mountain, both sides of the creek draining Mystery Lake, and Drystone Creek are enlivened each spring and summer with a profusion of delicate flowers. With more than 200 species of mountain flowers, the region rivals the nearby national park in its diversity and abundance of wild flowers. The orchid family is particularly well represented, with the Calypso, yellow lady's-slipper and sparrow's-egg orchids all found in this wilderness.

The traveller to the Folding Mountain

Clearcut logging to the east contrasts sharply with the alpine meadows that drape Folding Mountain and with the National Park wilderness to the west.

Wildland can also hope to glimpse the endangered peregrine falcon. The falcon, nearly eliminated throughout its former range by the introduction of DDT contaminants, visits the wilderness during its spring and fall migrations. Due to the protection offered by the adjacent

national park, the visitor may also see solitude-loving animals such as the grizzly bear and wolf.

Turbulent stream environments and cold temperatures keep fish productivity low. Although eastern brook trout and rainbow trout were stocked in Mystery Lake in three different years, neither species took, leaving the lake with only its native bull trout population. Drinnan Creek has a number of beaver ponds which provide suitable habitat for the rainbow and bull trout found along its length.

Recreation

Tucked in a corner formed by a main highway and a national park, Folding Mountain offers both accessibility and solitude, and provides a buffer between settled areas, transportation corridors and the protected wilderness of the Jasper National Park. This pocket wilderness is ideal for those looking for a challenging day trip, or a two to three day trip by horse, foot, or even snowshoe. The two most scenic routes involve the challenge of crossing the Fiddle River and its narrow canyon along the trail from Miette Hot Springs, or the challenge of travelling right over Folding Mountain peak south along the 16 kilometre trail from the Yellowhead Highway. Though National Parks relinquished the lands, the park service still maintains the 11.7 kilometre trail from Miette Hot Springs to Mystery Lake. A third access begins with dry weather roads leading west off the gravel road to Cadomin and makes use of the historic trail route up Drinnan Creek to Mystery Lake.

The top of Folding Mountain affords a view of contrasts. From a height of 2118 metres above sea level, one can compare the qualities of natural wilderness to the west with those of "developed" lands in the east. To the northwest, the Athabasca River valley is like an open door to the lush green forests and stunning peaks of Jasper National Park. In the east and southeast, a distant coal strip mine and a foreground of denuded blocks left by clearcut logging graphically depict the adjacent resource development.

Even though the natural productivity of fish is low, both Mystery Lake and Drinnan Creek provide high quality opportunities for the angler.

In 1984, two commercial outfitters were conducting operations in this wilderness area. One guides summer trips from a base near Miette Hot Springs, the other provides fall hunting trips from neighbouring provincial lands.

Vehicle access campgrounds along Highway 16 at Pocahontas inside Jasper Park, at a small private resort on the north boundary of the Wildland Recreation Area, and at a provincial campground further east towards Hinton, all provide suitable staging areas for trips into Folding Mountain. Once within the Wildland Recreation Area, the east end of Mystery Lake is an excellent camping spot.

Land Use Concerns and Recommendations

Although this proposed Wildland Recreation Area is just five kilometres across, only the western half, adjacent to the national park, is protected as Prime Protection lands. The remaining lands are zoned to permit the full range of resource development. The area immediately to the east side of Mystery Lake is zoned "Industrial Use" in order to permit the single use of coal development. Thus, Folding Mountain peak and most of the area traversed by the trail from the Yellowhead Highway to Mystery Lake presently fall outside the protective zoning under the province's Eastern Slopes Policy. This land use zoning is undergoing government review, which may result in more appropriate protection for Folding Mountain.

Coal, Oil and Gas

About 70 percent of the Folding Mountain Wildland is under coal lease, and strip mining is conducted in the Luscar coal fields to the southeast of the area. The eastern half of the Folding Mountain Wildland is presently zoned for coal development, which would permit exploration and underground mines or strip mines.

There are oil and gas leases in the proposed Wildland Recreation Area, and two exploratory wells have been drilled nearby. However, the Folding Mountain Wildland has low potential for these resources.

Timber

In 1972, the majority of the Folding Mountain wilderness was removed from the North West Pulp and Paper Timber Harvesting Agreement Area and placed under a provincial park reserve. Unfortunately, this was changed with the 1977 Eastern Slopes Policy, which would permit additional logging.

Given the area's small size, its intrinsic wild values and its location on the border of Jasper National Park, the choice should be made to protect this accessible wilderness garden.

White Goat
Regaining a Wilderness

When we finally stow the excess gear inside the truck, lock the door, turn the trussed and groaning pack string loose and swing up into the saddle, a great weight lifts from my shoulders. I turn my face and mind from the harried office and the buzzing highway and head west up a rugged valley flanked by sharp grey peaks. Soon all I hear and know is the clacking of horseshoes on stone, the rushing of water in the stream beside. Soon the pace of life is no longer measured by the watch, but by the step of the horse, by hunger pangs in the stomach, and the rise and fall of the sun. We adjust, and our senses fine tune to the immediate world unfolding around each bend in the trail.

The previous week of hectic preparations, when I swear I'll never again take on the responsibility of organizing a horse trip, is forgotten as the wind, the sun, the scenery and the kinship with fellow man and horses drown the memories. But without the endless lists and the careful preparation, a trip with horses can be fraught with misery. Before the first trip of the season, there's a long day with the ferrier, sweat pouring as he beats out the shoes to fit each impatient pony. Then a day to sort hobbles, bells, nose bags, halters, to mend a broken latigo, replace a fraying cinch, make sure the tent is waterproof, the saddle and rigging leather all rubbed with neatsfoot oil. A day is needed to plan the food, essential horse equipment, fly repellent, oats, penicillin,

extra shoes and personal gear, axe, saw, lantern, etc. A day is needed to shop and a day to pack, each hard item rolled in newspaper to prevent chaffing and breaking in the pack boxes as the ponies go through their antics on the trail. Each box is carefully balanced with its partner and a list of its contents tacked to the inner lid. It's a nuisance when you're starting out, but the careful organization pays dividends at the end of a long day with darkness approaching, horse tempers short, and humans ravenous. A copy of the horse-packer's bible, Joe Back's *Horses, Hitches and Rocky Trails,* goes into the saddle bag for a quick reference.

No matter what, you never get away early on the first day, so if your trip into the

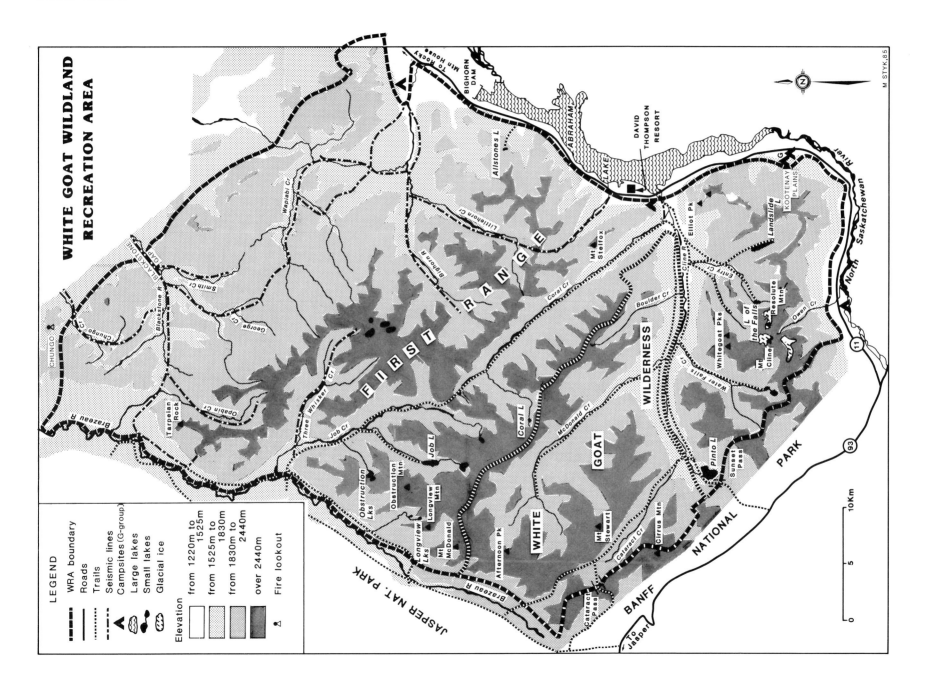

WHITE GOAT WILDLAND RECREATION AREA

LEGEND

WRA boundary
Roads
Trails
Seismic lines
Campsites (G-group)
Large lakes
Small lakes
Glacial ice

Elevation

from 1220m to 1525m
from 1525m to 1830m
from 1830m to 2440m
over 2440m

Fire lookout

M STYK, 85

White Goat Wildland Recreation Area begins at the mouth of Coral Creek on the David Thompson Highway, you know the first night will be spent somewhere in this narrow, rough, but splendid valley. Horse feed is scarce in Coral, so supplemental feed the first night is a good idea.

The hurtling stream and boulder-strewn bed of Coral Creek, with over 30 crossings of the horse trail along its length, is a challenge and a danger to those on foot, and necessitates care on horses. As the trail ascends Coral Creek valley, deep green tributary valleys, topped by red-streaked and snow-capped peaks, come into view, each inviting exploration. On a patch of green velvet on a pitched limestone face, a family of mountain goats may be glimpsed, serene in their kingdom high above us.

If the horses are in reasonable shape, we'll wend our way up Coral Creek for approximately 18 kilometres before we turn right and follow a tributary of Coral Creek that will allow us to traverse Job Pass before the end of the second day. The trail up to the pass is broad and worn as it rises through pine and spruce, breaking out into open willow, then into alpine meadows, usually dotted with bighorn lambs and ewes, as we approach Job Pass summit. From the pass, the entire lower Coral Creek valley can be seen, stretching to the North Saskatchewan River, the peaks of the Ram and Whiterabbit forming the horizon. Across the pass, Job Creek is a blue ribbon between meadowed banks, dwarfed by the grey slab of mountains on either side.

Descending into Job Valley is hazardous as the trail is steep and deeply rutted. Pack ponies do best when equipped with britchen to keep the loads from sliding over their heads. Usually packs and saddles need adjusting at the bottom. Job Valley is gentle relief, horse feed is plentiful and several old outfitters' camps make a delightful base for a few days of dayriding or exploration on two feet instead of four.

Job Lake, the jewel of the area, can be reached on horseback from a Job Valley base camp. Because the lake has a reputation for excellent cutthroat trout fishing, it has received excessive use, so it is inadvisable to plan your camp at this abused paradise, unless you are travelling on foot.

We often shift camp in Job Valley, setting base camp again after an easy day's ride down Job, then exploring more of the side valleys and craggy passes by foot. Vistas of range piled on range, verdant alpine basins of beauty unsurpassed in our Rockies, and herds of grazing bighorns reward the fatigued climber who achieves any of the high passes in the area.

If a party has spent time positioning vehicles before beginning a White Goat trip, several possibilities exist for continuing the trip out of Job Valley. From the junction of the Job with the Brazeau River, a party may travel on good trails up the Brazeau, crossing into Jasper Park and travelling up over Nigel or Jonas passes onto the Banff-Jasper Highway. Another option is to follow the Brazeau downstream, then turn east on horse trails, seismic roads and reclaimed industrial roads to the Blackstone Gap - a ride of about two

days. Either way, the scenery remains spectacular, the wildlife is plentiful, and when open, the fishing reasonable in the Brazeau. In addition, if you're lucky, elk, grizzly and wolves are often to be seen in the broad valley of the Brazeau.

Finally, the tent is lowered on the last morning, the pack boxes weighed for balance, and the diamond hitches set for the day out. For us, it's down the Brazeau, across Opabin Creek and out into the broad meadows of the Wapiabi and Blackstone. The Bighorn Range is shining before us and the long grassy slopes of the First Range sweep down into the Wapiabi behind us.

My little saddle mare's hoofs beat a rhythm on the hardened trail, and we seem to be flying past trees and over streams at the speed of light, so adjusted am I to the pace of life in the Whitegoat that moves with the speed of the changing seasons.

Many valleys of the White Goat Wildland sweep up to jagged, 3000 metre peaks, then crumble, blanketing mountain slopes with loose scree. Other mountainsides clothed with green mountain avens and heather meadows cradle tranquil cirque lakes. Cold, clear Pinto Lake at the base of 2500 metre mountains provides some of the province's best combination of scenic beauty and fishing. It's not surprising the area has been described in a study of park potential in the Ram/Cline area as " . . . probably the most beautiful, varied tract of country remaining east of the Continental Divide which has not been given any formal protection."

The Bighorn, Little Horn, and Coral valleys are exceptionally scenic with red-streaked mountains above sculptured gorges and waterfalls. The lower valleys are fringed with aspen, leading into spruce and pine forests. The broad grasslands that sweep down from the front ranges into the Wapiabi/Blackstone provide splendid wildlife habitat, and awesome scenery.

Cradling the designated White Goat Wilderness and abutting Jasper and Banff National Parks, the wildland enjoys relative seclusion while remaining accessible via a major highway, the David Thompson, which skirts its southern borders.

The story of the loss of formal wilderness protection for two-thirds of the White Goat Wilderness in 1971 is viewed by many as a tragedy. In 1961, 1259 square kilometres of this splendid rugged haunt of the mountain goat were set aside as a wilderness park under the Forest Reserves Act. When the White Goat Wilderness Park was placed under the new 1971 Wilderness Areas Act, it was reduced in size by two-thirds to meet the 373 square kilometre restriction of the new Act. This removed from protection many of the lands in today's proposed White Goat Wildland Recreation Area, an area of 806 square kilometres.

Mount Cline's perfect pinnacle rises 3360 metres, displaying ancient Precambrian rock on its lower slopes. At the headwaters of Coral and Job creeks, stone stripes formed by the freezing and thawing of rock are visible. Here, coarse rock has been separated from fine material, leaving a striped pattern on the landscape. Another geological phenomenon, Tarpeian Rock in the northern tip of the White Goat Wildland, was described by the Earl of Southesk in 1859 as being of "a most remarkable shape, resembling an immense square block of masonry . . . like an altar raised by the giants of old to some of the extinct gods."

With most of the landscape above 2000 metres elevation, vegetation is primarily alpine or subalpine. A number of plants rare or uncommon in Alberta can be found in the White Goat.

The proposed Wildland Recreation Area contains the watersheds of the Cline and Brazeau rivers, which empty into the North Saskatchewan River. Developers have selected the stunning landscape at the junction of the Cline and North Saskatchewan rivers on the edge of this wilderness for a planned luxury recreation-resort complex. If successful, the Odyssey complex could put pressure on the White Goat Wildland by inviting intense human activity and motorized use, even along main wildlife migratory routes.

The Alberta Wilderness Association believes protection for these wilderness lands must be regained. There are currently no conflicting land ownership or reservation claims to hamper their protection. The potential for resource extraction is low and the area is too rugged and isolated for timber harvesting. The area's greatest value to Albertans is in wilderness recreation.

Geological History

Throughout most of the Eastern Slopes of Alberta's Rockies, the extremely hard coarse-grained Precambrian "basement" formed 500 million years ago dominates. Precambrian rock, for example, forms the base of Mount Cline in the White Goat. This ancient rock was pushed to the earth's surface by the upheavals which formed the Rocky Mountains. Elsewhere, massive blocks of rock hardened over the ages into the sandstone, shale, limestone and dolomite rock prevalent in the area. The faults along which the rock slid often cannot be detected by untrained observers. Geologists, however, have discovered two major faults extending through the White Goat: the McConnell Thrust northeast of Job Creek and the Pyramid Thrust west of Coral Creek. The mountains along these faults, which form part of the front range of the Rockies, are rugged and angular, and often streaked red by dissolved iron salts.

The landscape of the White Goat was altered further by at least two major glacial advances. The most recent began at the Continental Divide perhaps as late as 20,000 years ago. Ice blanketed the land to a thickness of 2500 metres, scouring and scraping the rock as it slid slowly eastward through major valleys. The glaciers widened these valleys and left their cargo of rock, gravel and till throughout low-lying areas of the Wildland Recreation Area. Cline River, Job Creek and Coral Creek cut through these mounds of glacial debris, exposing cliff faces

FACING PAGE: *Fireweed adds a flame of colour spreading up the Littlehorn Valley.* LEFT: *Job Lake, one of several fragile alpine tarns in the White Goat.* ABOVE: *A pack train making its way between Opabin and George Creeks.*

of boulders and pebbles. Some small glaciers remain in alpine areas of the Cline River's headwaters. Cirques and cirque lakes or tarns scooped out of mountainsides by glaciers, are common in this wilderness. Landslide Lake, Lake of the Falls, Pinto Lake, Wilson Lakes and Obstruction Lakes are all tarns.

Human History

The Kootenay, Peigan and Stoney Indians knew the White Goat well. The land of the White Goat was traditionally Kootenay. In the early 1800s, the Stoney tribes moved into the White Goat to hunt.

The famous Northwest Company fur trader David Thompson used the North Saskatchewan River valley just south of the White Goat as a main trade route until he was forced into discovering the Athabasca Pass further north when his preferred route, the Howse Pass on the North Saskatchewan, was closed by the Peigans to stop white men from trading muskets to the Kootenay tribes.

Duncan McGillivary, another famous fur trader, probably entered the White Goat in 1800 while en route to the Brazeau River on the western boundary of the Wildland Recreation Area. The Kootenay Indians frequently used a trail along the Cline River in this wilderness to travel between the Kootenay Plains and the Jasper House trading post.

In 1859, James Carnegie, the sporting Earl of Southesk, travelled up the Brazeau Valley to the Job Creek area where he and his guides wandered, lost, until they found an exit to the North Saskatchewan River. He described Coral Valley as " . . . enclosed by a precipitous wall of mountains of pearly grey colour, composed of hard stone lying in layers like a slate cut in diamond shape."

A.P. Coleman, a professor of geology at the University of Toronto, traversed the area five times between 1892 and 1902 en route to higher mountains to the northwest. He named Pinto Lake after his troublesome horse.

The adventurous Mary Schaeffer, a wealthy Quaker from Pennsylvania, travelled through the area at the beginning of the 20th century during her excursions to Jasper National Park. Widowed in her thirties, she spent summers exploring western mountains in spite of protests from disbelieving family and friends.

In the early 1900s, the Water Survey of Canada and the Geological Survey of Canada prepared field reports from the Brazeau and Cline valleys, and the Topographical Surveys Branch was in the area in 1927. To accommodate these activities, trails and simple cabins were built. The entire Wildland Recreation Area was then part of a forest reserve managed by the federal government for watershed protection. In 1930 the Wildland became part of the Clearwater Forest, to be managed by the Province of Alberta. The provincial government initially maintained trails in the area, some of which have been kept clear by local outfitters.

A boreal owl at home in an old growth forest in the White Goat Wildland.

Wildlife

The protection afforded wildlife in the adjoining Banff and Jasper National Parks and White Goat Wilderness Area helps maintain sheep and goat populations throughout the area.

Many of the White Goat Wildland's estimated 450 sheep graze on sunny, south-facing slopes in the Cline River valley, along the First Range near the mouth of the Cline River, and at Tarpeian Rock, Obstruction Mountain and in the Job and Coral Creek valleys. Mountain goats often range in the Coral Creek region as well as at Pinto and

Wilson lakes and the upper reaches of nearby McDonald Creek.

The Cline valley and the Blackstone, Brazeau and Wapiabi areas are popular for elk, but further west the generally rugged terrain and lack of suitable grazing areas limit elk populations. To the east, the Wapiabi/ Blackstone area provides choice ungulate habitat. Mule deer are sometimes seen along the Cline and Brazeau valleys; moose frequent valley bottoms along the Brazeau, in upper Coral Creek and in mid-Job Creek; and mountain caribou occur in some subalpine meadows, particularly around Pinto Lake. Now uncommon in Alberta, the mountain caribou are near the southern limit of their range in the White Goat. Mountain caribou, unlike barren ground caribou, do not migrate great distances, preferring to graze on alpine meadows around Cataract Pass until the autumn, when they move to the shelter of nearby old growth forests and valleys to feed on tree lichens, and willow tips through the winter. If stock animals become available, a program of introducing more mountain caribou into the ideal range in this region will be considered.

The wildlife habitat within the region was reduced with the construction of the David Thompson Highway and, later, the Bighorn dam on the North Saskatchewan River which flooded most of the Kootenay Plains. The remaining Kootenay Plains are an important wintering range for many of the area's elk, deer, moose and bighorn sheep.

Grizzlies, wolverines, wolves and cougars are true wilderness animals, and require large tracts of undisturbed land. They find adequate habitat in the White Goat Wildland. Small animals typical of the Eastern Slopes, from fishers, lynx, marten and mink to northern flying squirrels, pikas and packrats, also live in the White Goat.

Year-round winged residents include spruce grouse, gray jay, Clarke's nutcracker, white-tailed ptarmigan, rosy finch and the dipper, which is often found nesting behind waterfalls. Migrant summer visitors include the waxwings, yellow warbler, pine siskin, rufous hummingbird, golden eagle, mountain bluebird, yellow-rumped warbler, water pipit, goldeneye and sandpipers.

Vegetation

The White Goat Wildland Recreation Area is high country, clothed in alpine and subalpine vegetation. Black spruce and muskeg characterize poorly drained areas while aspen poplar and balsam poplar persist on gravelled riverside flats and alluvial fans. Stream headwaters have meadows of willow, bog birch and sedge, while in Wilson and Job Creek valleys and the upper portions of the Brazeau Valley grasslands can be found.

Fire has influenced this wilderness, especially along the Cline River, where lodgepole pine regrowth replaces spruce and alpine fir. The pine shelters hairy wild rye as well as buffalo-berry, bearberry, Labrador tea, wild rose and juniper bushes.

Engelmann and white spruce mix with alpine fir in subalpine zones where buffalo-berry, green-alder, heather, twin-flower, Hedysarum, wild gooseberry, crowberry, bunchberry and feather mosses cover the forest floor.

Above elevations of 2000 meters, the forest thins. Trees which defy the elements at this altitude are wind-whipped, twisted and dwarfed. This is the Krummholz zone, an area of transition between subalpine forest and the dry tundra of the higher alpine regions. Ascending above the Krummholz zone, stunted alpine fir or spruce give way to hardy bearberry, mountain avens, willow, glacier lilies, buttercups, Indian paintbrush, cinquefoil and mountain heathers. Generally, alpine landscapes of the proposed White Goat Wildland Recreation Area are barren and rock-studded, although extensive alpine tundra exists in the upper Bighorn, Little Horn, Job and Coral drainages. Deep, loose scree blankets many mountain slopes.

An estimated 21 rare and 22 uncommon plants to Alberta have been recognized in subalpine and alpine areas of the adjacent White Goat Wilderness. Most of these plants occur in the proposed Wildland Recreation Area, including colonies of Lapland rose-bay, a species uncommon in Alberta. Growing on west-facing slopes near Job and Obstruction lakes, the upper Bighorn and the Sunset Pass area, the Lapland rose-bay can be recognized by its pinkish, azalea-type flowers and dark green, scaled leaves. It flowers briefly in late June, so its lovely display is rarely seen. Other rare or uncommon plant species include Rocky Mountain willowherb, purple alpine fleabane, cliff Romanzoffia and varieties of gentian and lousewort.

Recreation

Along with the watershed and wildlife habitat, recreation is the most important value of the proposed White Goat Wildland Recreation Area. The region has been appreciated for its beauty since man first ventured there, and today has a reputation as a fine hiking, trail riding, hunting and fishing area.

Hiking

Most established trails were blazed many years ago by Indians who hunted in this wilderness. These trails are generally long and rigorous, often requiring much stream fording. Prior to 1930, the Dominion Forest Service cut most of the trails along the major valleys. Some of these are today maintained by outfitters and the Alberta Forest Service. Some valleys, such as upper Coral Creek and parts of the Job trail, are open, providing panoramic views of surrounding landscapes. Backpacking is possible in Coral, Cline, Blackstone and Wapiabi valleys as well as the alpine area south of the Cline River. These trails are often steep and require numerous fords. Cline Crossing is the staging area most often used for extended trips into this wilderness. Further north, Blackstone Gap and Crescent Falls on the Bighorn River offer alternative entry points into lower elevation and gentler parts of the proposed Wildland Recreation Area.

The rugged nature, the largely unmaintained trails and the unpredictability of the weather mean that those planning extended trips into this area should be fit and familiar with true wilderness travel. Compasses and topographic maps are a must.

Backpacking trails in the upper Bighorn valley, Little Horn Creek and Cline Creek are unmaintained or non-existent. The terrain is very rough but the trip features splendid scenery. Headwater streams of the Bighorn River and Littlehorn Creek boast superb, steep-walled amphitheatres or cirques, many of which reveal the work of recent glaciation. Sedge meadows carpet upper valleys, and elk and bighorn sheep can often be seen feeding among the willows that line stream channels. In the lower valley are the spectacular Bighorn Gorge and Crescent Falls, surrounded by aspen and spruce forest.

Trail Riding

For many of the White Goat's trails, horseback is the most appropriate mode of travel because of the rugged nature of the terrain, the length of trails and the necessity of frequent creek fording. Valley bottom trails are replete with boulder-filled stream crossings.

There are suitable locations for horse camps but many of those which do exist are currently heavily used, and conflicts between horse grazing and wildlife are increasing. Serious consideration should be given to packing in supplemental horse feed, especially if a party is planning to camp near Job Lake or in the Coral Valley.

One favourite route follows the south side of Cline River west from Cline Crossing for about 32 kilometres to spectacular Pinto Lake. The Cline Trail also connects with destinations like Lake of the Falls, Landslide Lake and Shoeleather Creek trails. The 50 kilometre Coral/Job Trail is a challenging two-day trip from Cline Crossing to Job Lake. Down Job Creek, the trail links with the South Boundary Trail into Jasper National Park, or with a low, somewhat boggy trail, down the Brazeau, across the broad plains of the Wapiabi to Blackstone Gap.

Mountaineering

Because of their loose scree slopes, many of the mountains in the Wildland Recreation Area are dangerous, but not necessarily technically challenging. The Alpine Club of Canada recognizes three areas as significant for climbing:

- South of Cline River on Mount Cline, White Goat, Sentinel and Resolute mountains.

- Mount Stewart, Afternoon Peak, Mount MacDonald and Obstruction Mountain.

- The White Goat, Lion, Lioness and Sentinel mountains and other challenging lower peaks near Windy Point in the First Range that are all between 3000 and 3400 metres in elevation.

Several first ascents are still possible in parts of this wilderness.

Camping

Vehicle staging areas occur at Cline River crossing, Blackstone Gap and Crescent Falls on the Bighorn River. Primitive campsites for hikers and trail riders have been established through random use at Pinto Lake and Job Lake as well as at many stream junctions and trail forks.

Hunting and Fishing

The native bull trout are common in the North Saskatchewan drainage, including the Brazeau drainage, lower reaches of Cline and Coral creeks, MacDonald and Cataract creeks and in Pinto Lake. Rocky Mountain whitefish have been introduced in the area and along with bull trout are common in the Brazeau drainage as well as in lower reaches of Cline and Coral creeks. Native cutthroat trout have been introduced into the lower Bighorn River, Lake of the Falls, Landslide and Job lakes as well as in numerous unnamed high lakes west of Mount Cline. Golden trout have been stocked in Michelle and Coral lakes. Rainbow trout are present in the Brazeau drainage.

Pinto Lake, long renowned for its bull trout fishing, is still visited by local Indians who net a winter's catch. Competition with fishermen helicoptered in may now pose major use problems at this resilient lake, and will certainly detract from its wilderness appeal.

One of the most popular longstanding recreation activities in the White Goat is hunting. Sheep, elk and bear as well as moose are available in this area. Elk inhabit a wide area of this wilderness but generally avoid the most rugged terrain in favor of forested valleys with open grasslands. Both sheep and goats inhabit the highest peaks and hanging valleys of the White Goat Wildland which provide prime range in the upper reaches of Coral Creek and near Pinto Lake. The south-facing slopes of the Cline River valley are particularly favourable for sheep.

The Cline and Coral valleys were once part of the designated White Goat Wilderness Area until the Wilderness Areas Act of 1971 forced size limitations on these areas. In the White Goat Wilderness Area, now basically the MacDonald Creek valley, fishing, hunting and horse use are prohibited. Sheep and goat flourish in the area and often move into adjacent watersheds such as the proposed Wildland Recreation Area, where hunting is permitted.

Land Use Concerns and Recommendations

Although one-third of this wilderness is forested, most of the timber is where steep slopes, loose soil and watershed values demand its exclusion from timber cutting. Some merchantable stands in the lower Bighorn and Wapiabi drainages are slated for harvest and will undoubtedly prove controversial in the future.

During the oil and gas bonanza of the mid-1950s, several seismic lines were cut through the White Goat and along the Brazeau River's south bank, the lower Job and Three Whisker Creek. Extensive exploration occurred in the Wapiabi and Bighorn drainages. Eleven field parties examined the area for its oil and gas potential in the 1950s, and in 1969 an access road was constructed to a test well on Opabin Creek. The road has since been reclaimed.

A coal formation was discovered about eight miles east of the Wildland Recreation Area in the Bighorn Range but access is limited by the nature of the terrain. To their very headwaters both the Bighorn and Little Horn drainages bear scars of past seismic activities. No reclamation work has been done on these roads.

Fishermen are being flown by helicopter into Job or Wilson Lake, Obstruction Lake, Pinto Lake and Landslide Lake, causing concern to those who enjoy the isolation and solitude of the White Goat, and the wilderness experience it can so richly provide.

The proposed four season Odyssey development, a conference/resort complex, could also threaten the wild character of this entire area. A site near the Abraham Reservoir abutting the White Goat Wilderness has been chosen for the complex. The AWA, as well as other organizations and nearby residents of the Indian reserve and Rocky Mountain House, are concerned about the effect such a commercial development could have on the wilderness character of nearby lands. Construction and increased human activity as well as increased hunting and fishing pressure would adversely affect wildlife populations. Environmental and economic concerns have currently led to the death of the project.

Ram/Whiterabbit
Expansive Uplands

One of the truly gentle wilderness hikes in Alberta's Eastern Slopes is the Ram/Whiterabbit. It was July 10th and we were assembling our backpacks at the junction of Canary Creek and the Onion Lake road just west of Ram Falls. With nine days of food and lightweight gear, six of us were "escorted" five kilometres up Canary Creek by a four wheel drive and several dirt bikes despite an earth barrier and signs contary to their access. Fortunately, the road became a trail and we left the noise and dust behind.

We camped at the Canary Creek headwaters. It snowed that night, collapsing the tents. This dubious beginning, however, heralded the start of seven glorious days of sunshine. The following day, we continued over to the Ram River and up to Headwater cabin, and then went west to an outfitter's camp. Next morning as we continued upstream, we rounded a corner and, there in the distance, was a startling black and white stone outcrop. Closer examination showed it to be a mass of white quartz-impregnated coral fossils embedded in jet black rock. Beyond this, the trail abruptly ended at a 25 metre cliff band and waterfall. Scouting ahead for a route we startled a band of bighorn ewes. Effortlessly, they scaled a scree slope and kindly showed us a route through the cliff band. It was not a route we wanted to take with backpacks, however, so we turned back, disappointed. On the descent, I got a glimpse of a fossil. It was a near perfect trilobite. In the next half-hour we discovered others in an area so rich we were discarding poor ones for perfect.

Over lunch, as we pondered our dilemma over the route, a poignant drama unfolded before us on the edge of a gorge and waterfall. A ptarmigan mother startled by another band of sheep flew across the ravine, leaving three very excited chicks on the "wrong" side. One chick took courage, and flew through the mist of the canyon to its mother's side. A second chick flew but the vortex winds of the waterfall sucked it down into the falls, leaving a third, very distraught chick calling and pacing. Nearly one-half hour elapsed before it made a successful attempt. We wondered aloud what the original size of this tiny family had been.

Our decision was to backpack to Headwaters cabin and then follow the main branch of the South Ram. From a base camp we explored a series of unnamed lakes surrounded by rugged meadow-covered ridges dotted with over one hundred bighorns. The following day, we investigated the headwaters of the Ram River and the Ram Glacier, finding to our surprise a glacier research team's A-frame in a spectacular ice and moraine setting. Traversing the ice and surrounding ridges gave us views into the Clearwater River, down Escarpment Creek and into the Siffleur.

Our return trip to Canary Creek over Indian Head Pass and Ranger Creek was slightly longer than our route in. Few areas in the Eastern Slopes can match the beauty of this broad green subalpine pass. We climbed out of the valley in the rich light of the setting sun, camping on the edge of the alpine reaches of Ranger Creek. This part of the Eastern Slopes is easy to negotiate with or without a trail, making it perfect for cross-country travel. For the next two days we hopped from the Ranger drainage over a Scotland-like meadow onto the Ram and finally up and past ridges of eerie black-and-silver-bleached fire-scarred trees to Canary Creek. During a rest stop in the meadow, amongst the scarlet Indian paintbrush and brilliant yellow stonecrop we found an incandescent light bulb – a grim reminder that below in Canary Creek was the end of our trip, the van and the Buck Rogers

RIGHT: *Prime wildlife habitat gently molded in the head waters of Scalp Creek.*

crowd. Where in North America can one experience such high quality uncrowded wilderness recreation? The Ram/Whiterabbit is worthy of its Prime Protection Zoning and our continued protective vigilance.

W ind whistles through the broad valleys, across extensive alpine grasslands and bald, high-rolling foothills of the Ram/ Whiterabbit Wildland. To the west, the mountains of Banff National Park tower over the landscape.

Spread between the North Saskatchewan and Red Deer rivers, the Ram/Whiterabbit's watershed provides clean, consistent quantities of water to points as far away as Prince Albert, Saskatchewan.

The northern tip of the Wildland is almost 200 kilometres west of the city of Red Deer. Some 24 times larger than the city, the Wildland is a popular recreation area for the residents of Red Deer, Rocky Mountain House and Edmonton.

Seventeen hundred square kilometres in area, the Ram/Whiterabbit is high quality wilderness. This wilderness area has been spared major disruption by humans because it lacks large quantities of marketable timber, oil, gas or coal. Two hard-surface roads and a gravel road approach the boundaries of the Wildland, but no open roads interrupt its interior. Grizzly bear, cougar and wolf require large tracts of undisturbed territory. In the Ram/Whiterabbit, these animals are able to

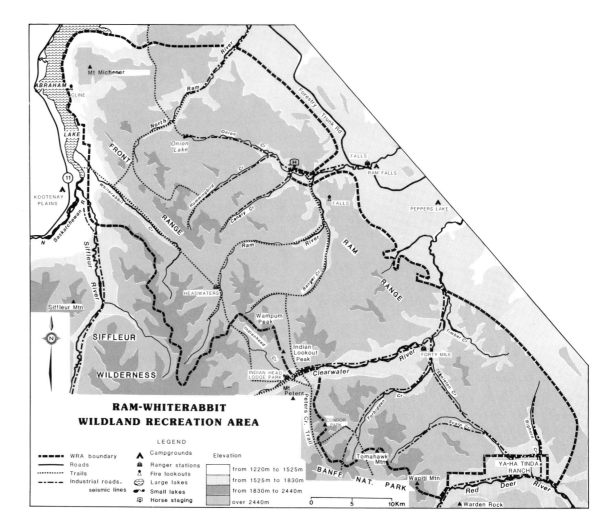

RAM-WHITERABBIT WILDLAND RECREATION AREA

LEGEND

- ▲ Campgrounds
- ⌂ Ranger stations
- ⚓ Fire lookouts
- Large lakes
- Small lakes
- Horse staging

WRA boundary
Roads
Trails
Industrial roads, seismic lines

Elevation
from 1220m to 1525m
from 1525m to 1830m
from 1830m to 2440m
over 2440m

0   5   10Km

maintain healthy populations. Alberta Fish and Wildlife, recognizing the area's importance for wildlife, strives to ensure that the prime grasslands are maintained. Cattle grazing is not permitted and resource extraction is discouraged or carefully monitored through most of this area in order to preserve wildlife habitat.

The proposed Wildland is adjacent to land already under protection as the Siffleur Wilderness and Banff National Park. The grassland of the Kootenay Plains, just northwest of the Wildland, is a valuable wildlife range and is a candidate for Ecological Reserve designation. A flat, wind-dried prairie in the midst of a relatively humid mountain region, the plains provide an important migration corridor and grazing range for wildlife, particularly elk. The Siffleur Wilderness at the Ram/Whiterabbit's northwest border has been given absolute protection under Alberta's Wilderness Areas Act. The southwest corner of the Wildland shares a boundary with Banff National Park, and to the south the Wildland abuts the government-owned Ya Ha Tinda Ranch. Because of its location, the proposed Ram/Whiterabbit Wildland could provide a buffer for several protected areas while offering opportunities for wilderness recreation.

Geological History

In the Ram/Whiterabbit Wildland, there is evidence of ages past. Imbedded in the shale, limestone and sandstone of the area are fossilized trilobites and primitive crustaceans from the bottom of quiet ancient seas; coal from compressed debris of sub-tropical, prehistoric swamps; faulted and folded rock from the era of mountain building. The Devonian-era fossils and shelf outcroppings at Hummingbird Creek near the Wildland's eastern border attract many visitors. The Hummingbird Creek fossils are similar in age and structure to the petroleum-rich reef reservoirs of Alberta's plains and foothills and are of great interest to geologists.

The Ram Range on the west side of the proposed Wildland is part of the front range of the Rocky Mountains. This range displays some of the oldest rocks in North America. The earth's turmoil during mountain building is imprinted in the ridges of the Ram Range and the twisted rock of Devil's Porridge, a cliff at the confluence of Ram River and Hummingbird Creek just east of the Ram/Whiterabbit Wildland.

Glaciers also shaped the terrain, leaving behind bare, rock-strewn mountainside basins or cirques, dammed by their own debris. More than 10,000 years ago, glacial meltwater wore sharp V-shaped furrows into the rock. As the ice moved eastward, it scoured and widened valleys and deposited rocks and till in low-lying areas. Beyond the Wildland area, the Gap, where the North Saskatchewan River thunders through the Brazeau Range, was carved by glaciers.

Waterfalls along most of the major rivers in the area, with their tiered rock and narrow gorges, are the product of erosion on layers of rock of varying hardness. Fast-moving creeks carry and drop gravel and silt as they slow down on level terrain, producing alluvial fans throughout the Wildland. Examples of these gravel flats can be found along the North Ram and at Whiterabbit Creek and Siffleur River where they enter the North Saskatchewan River at the northwest edge of the Wildland Recreation Area.

Human History

Through the ages, the North Saskatchewan River, along the Wildland's northwest boundary, has attracted prehistoric people, fur traders and explorers. The river's wide valley, relatively mild climate and abundant wildlife brought hunting peoples to the area as long ago as 8,000 years. Large herds of buffalo, elk and bighorns once roamed the grasslands of the North Saskatchewan corridor, and there were a number of hunting camps in the valley.

The Kootenay Indians travelled the North Saskatchewan River valley to reach trading posts along the river. They called the valley "Kadoona Tinda" or "Windy Plains". Today the valley just to the west of the Ram/Whiterabbit is known as the Kootenay Plains. Within the proposed Wildland, the Clearwater Valley has the only sound archaeological evidence of significant prehistoric human use.

In his search for a pass through the Great Divide, David Thompson in 1801 explored the Ram/Whiterabbit, following the North Saskatchewan Valley just to the north, and used it to meet Kootenay Indians with whom he traded. But Peigan Indians, jealous of the trading alliance between Thompson and the Kootenays, frequently blocked the corridors to fur traders.

Interest in the North Saskatchewan corridor

diminished after the discovery of the Athabasca Pass. One year after Thompson's death in 1857, James Hector, a geologist with the Palliser Expedition, travelled in the Kootenay Plains using Stoney Indian guides. The Stoneys were perhaps the forerunners of a group that left their Morley Reserve in 1892 to start anew on the Kootenay Plains. A reserve was later established for the band on the Bighorn River, and reserve residents still hunt in the proposed Ram/ Whiterabbit Wildland. Their original wagon trail can still be followed to Nordegg. In the mid-1960s the Smallboy group from Hobbema's Ermineskin band moved to the Kootenay Plains. But their dream of escaping the white man's world lost its lustre and they abandoned their camp in the early 1970s.

In 1902, Tom Wilson, a well known guide and outfitter in central Alberta, established a horse ranch near the mouth of Whiterabbit Creek, just northwest of the Wildland. In 1911 the provincial government acquired Wilson's ranch and moved the old buildings to another property across the North Saskatchewan River. The area is today flooded by the backwater of the Bighorn Dam. Construction of the dam in 1969 was only the beginning of recent changes imposed on the impressive Kootenay Plains and surrounding wildlands.

Wildlife and Vegetation

Plants and animals of the Ram/Whiterabbit are fairly typical of central Alberta's Eastern Slopes.

Dense forests of lodgepole pine and white spruce blanket lower elevations, shading an understory of green alder, buffalo-berry, juniper, bearberry, hairy wild rye and mosses. A few wet areas, particularly along streams, are vegetated with black spruce, sphagnum moss, willow and sedge. Generally, however, there is little suitable low-elevation habitat for moose and mule deer. The Clearwater and Red Deer River valleys are

migratory routes for elk which travel through the Wildland each autumn. Elk, deer and small bands of feral horses winter in the Wildland's lower valleys.

As in most recently burned Eastern Slopes regions, Engelmann spruce and lodgepole pine dominate elevations above 1700 metres. Typical examples of this zone occur in the upper drainage of the Ram and North Ram rivers, where open

FACING PAGE: *The high country of Ranger Creek, a setting for one of the Ram/ Whiterabbit's leisurely trips.* LEFT: *A colour-splashed subalpine meadow in the head of the North Ram River.* ABOVE: *A camp on the watershed divide between the North Ram River and Whiterabbit Creek.*

stands of spruce with bearberry, creeping juniper, Labrador tea, mosses, lichens and low bilberry clothe dry, rocky slopes.

The subalpine zone occurs at about 2000 metres where alpine fir dominates. Grouseberry, white mountain heather and yellow heather form the understory here.

Grassy plateaus between the Ram and North Ram rivers are home to an estimated 600 bighorn sheep, as well as mountain goats. Natural salt licks in the proposed Wildland Recreation Area at Scalp Creek are an attraction to many sheep. There is a significant black bear population in the Wildland and cougars, grizzly bears and wolves can sometimes be seen. The Wildland Recreation Area is also home to coyotes, marmots, grouse, birds of prey and songbirds. Several trappers work the area for the fur bearing mammals including wolves and wolverines.

A transition Krummholz zone occurs at the treeline where stunted fir and spruce stands brave the elements. The climate is harsh and snow often remains until August in high mountainside cirques or basins.

The shores of icy cirque lakes are enlivened by colourful flowers such as mountain marigold, globe-flower and elephant head as well as sedges, sphagnum mosses and willows. Dry, windy plateaus of alpine regions invite the growth of Kobresia, mountain avens, shrubby cinquefoil, lousewort, yellow heather and Indian paintbrush. The spider plant, rare in Alberta, can be recognized in some high alpine reaches by its yellow flowers and smooth, whip-like runners. The delicate alpine poppy can be found on the highest exposed tundra areas. On exposed sunny shoulders, the rare and beautiful shrub Lapland rose-bay is occasionally found.

Recreation

The Ram/Whiterabbit Wildland is not a notably productive area for fish. Most streams move fast; water volumes fluctuate dramatically and eroding stream banks deposit silt which limits fish habitat. There are, however, several waterways stocked with cutthroat trout, including Ranger, Hummingbird, Canary and Onion creeks.

Recently, adverse water conditions during spawning have curtailed cutthroat populations in the Ram River. In response, Alberta Fish and Wildlife has imposed an experimental catch-and-release program. Rather than closing the river to sport fishing, anglers may fish using barbless hooks, providing they release their catches. Introduced in 1982, the program will continue until fish populations stabilize. Bull trout and Rocky Mountain whitefish spawn and overwinter primarily in the Clearwater River and some of its tributaries.

The area produces many record-book trophy bighorn sheep. Fall guided outfitting has a long-established presence in the area, with elk, moose, grizzly, wolf and bighorn sheep being sought. The small goat population in the wilderness has been totally protected since 1969.

Hiking and Trail Riding

Old Indian trails, outfitters' trails and seismic lines are the most widely used routes in the Wildland. Some follow the flat-floored valleys of Onion and Hummingbird creeks as well as upper sections of the Ram River, the North Ram, Clearwater River, Forbidden Creek, Scalp Creek

and Ranger Creek. Vegetation along these routes is not dense and the view of surrounding mountains is largely uninterrupted. High plateaus and alpine meadows provide variety and excellent skyline views. Several trails continue into Banff National Park and the Siffleur Wilderness Area, providing opportunities for extended trips. Recommended short trips include those along the gorge of the Ram River and Hummingbird Creek. Off-highway vehicle use occurs on seismic lines in the Ram drainage but currently the Ram/Whiterabbit is relatively undisturbed.

In the Scalp, Forbidden and Clearwater drainages, however, rampant off-road vehicle use has caused both physical and aesthetic deterioration of the terrain. As a result, the provincial government called for abandoned seismic lines and industrialized roads to be closed to motorized use. It is expected that almost all of the Ram/Whiterabbit will fall under legislation protecting it against vehicle use in the near future.

The Ram/Whiterabbit area is ideal for extended horse packing trips, and with protection could continue to provide this traditional enjoyment for generations to come.

Camping

The Kootenay Plains Natural Area is heavily used as a vehicle camping and staging area for extended trips. As a proposed Ecological Reserve, however, the area should not be subject to intensive use. Alternative staging or vehicle camping areas include the North Ram River Crossing, the Ram River/Hummingbird Creek junction, and the Ya Ha Tinda Ranch area. Back country camping opportunities abound for horse and foot travellers in the Wildland Recreation Area.

Cross-country skiing is limited in the proposed Wildland because of the expansive wind-blown terrain and highly variable snow conditions. Outside the Wildland, the Ram River provides challenging canoe and kayak courses.

Land Use Concerns and Recommendations

The Ram/Whiterabbit is most valued for its wildlife habitat, recreational opportunities and watershed importance. The area is also an important buffer for Banff National Park, the Siffleur Wilderness Area and the proposed Kootenay Plains Ecological Reserve.

The terrain of the 412-square-kilometre Siffleur Wilderness Area is similar to that on the west side of the Ram/Whiterabbit. It is hoped that, like the Siffleur Wilderness, the proposed Wildland Recreation Area would be out-of-bounds to motorized vehicles, resource exploration and development.

However, unlike the Siffleur, the AWA's proposed Wildland Recreation Area would include managed hunting, fishing and horse use. It is the destruction and disruption of wildlife habitat through resource exploration activities and vehicle use, not hunting, that presents the greatest threat to wildlife populations. The Alberta Forest Service in 1983 had to block access to motorized vehicles in the Scalp/

Clearwater area because of disruption caused by indiscriminate use by off-road vehicles. Forest Land Use Zone designations are expected to finally allow a legal means of regulating both vehicle and horse use of much of the Wildland Recreation Area proposal.

Wildlife populations in the Wildland, like those in the proposed White Goat Wildland Recreation Area, declined as a result of the construction of the David Thompson Highway along the major winter ranges of the Kootenay Plains. Flooding of nearby grazing land by the Bighorn Dam compounded the problem.

Long before construction of the Bighorn Dam in 1969, the Eastern Rockies Forest Conservation Board recognized the importance of the region as a natural area. It stated, "The headwaters of the Ram River has so many characteristics that make it an ideal wilderness area that its possibilities should be given serious consideration… Important watershed values could be protected under the wilderness concept."

Today, in 1986, the area is still in need of protection.

Oil, Gas and Coal

About 20 percent of the Wildland is under oil and gas lease, and resource exploration has been conducted on the east side of the Wildland as well as in the south, where seismic lines and abandoned well sites intrude. However, the petroleum potential of the area is considered low.

Although the Ram/Whiterabbit is in Category I in Alberta's Coal Policy, which recommends against coal exploration or

extraction, about one-fifth of this wilderness is under coal lease. These leases are not likely to be renewed upon expiration.

Logging

The only areas with potential for commercial forestry are on the Clearwater River, the Bighorn River, and in the area just east of the Wildland proposal along the Ram River. At present, most of this timber is not mature enough for harvesting. There are no proposals for cutting along the Clearwater River, and the Eastern Slopes Policy recommends no commercial logging in the high country of this proposed Wildland Recreation Area.

Trapping

There are eight registered traplines in the area which produce well. Trapping is a use which is compatible with the proposed Wildland Recreation Area.

Panther Corners
High Country Grasslands

M y aching legs clung desperately to the galloping mare who was rushing headlong down the Panther River valley toward camp at the confluence with the Dormer River valley. There she would find rest and food. Heaven knew I could use that too. We had ridden seven hours over rugged mountain trails - torture to the lower anatomy of the novice horsewoman.

Despite the physical agony, I felt ecstatic. My three companions and I had seen a great deal of the Panther Corners wilderness on horseback in the last few days. The experience had renewed my ties with nature in all its autumn splendour. It had refreshed a spirit dulled by too many days in offices and boardrooms.

The first day after establishing camp, we had checked out reclamation of a wellsite and access road in the dense lodgepole pine forests east of camp and Dogrib Creek. Although the scars would be there for many years, the manner in which reclamation had been accomplished ensured no further disruption by off-road vehicles. It was heartening to see this care being taken by a large corporation.

Next day we had ridden north along Dogrib Creek and had climbed a spur ridge of Jap Mountain. From the top, we gazed north across

From the rugged mountains of Banff National Park Wilderness, backpackers study maps, planning a looped route eastward into the Panther Corners Wildland Recreation Area.

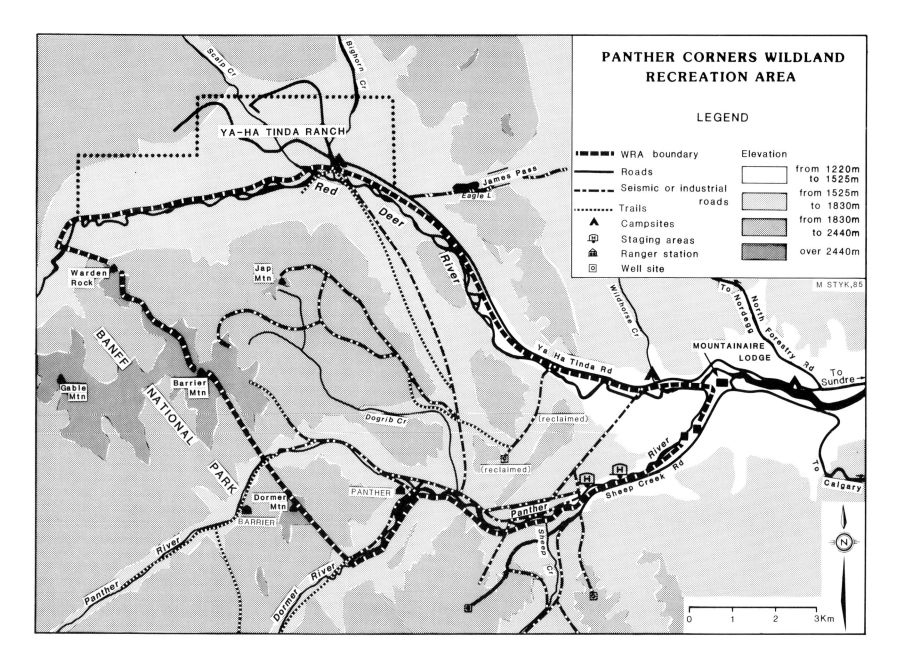

PANTHER CORNERS WILDLAND
RECREATION AREA

LEGEND

▄▄ ▄▄ ▄▄	WRA boundary
———	Roads
—·—·—	Seismic or industrial roads
·······	Trails
▲	Campsites
🏢	Staging areas
⌂	Ranger station
⊡	Well site

Elevation

from 1220m to 1525m
from 1525m to 1830m
from 1830m to 2440m
over 2440m

M STYK,85

the broad Red Deer River valley to the open plains of the Ya Ha Tinda Ranch. The warm chinook winds which blew freshness and energy into my soul had over the years blown these south-facing ridges and plains into grasslands which remained free of snow during winters, enabling large herds of elk from Banff National Park to survive the winter there. Signs of their winter ranges linger in the form of hardened pellets, bits of hair and bleached antlers. Another month or two and the elk would be returning.

Today we had ridden southwest along the braided Dormer River into the backcountry of Banff National Park. An old horse trail led north over a low pass west of Dormer Mountain, between the Dormer and Panther rivers. At the summit of the pass, we had lunched in an open meadow and, anxious to stretch cramped leg muscles, had climbed a rocky ridge. The view from the top was glorious. We could look southward to Panther Mountain at the northern end of the rugged Palliser Range, westward to the snow-capped Bare Mountains which hid the Continental Divide from our view, and northward to the gentle ridges of alternating grass and forest which lay between the Panther and Red Deer rivers. From that eagles' perch we schemed, dreaming about other mountains we could climb, other valleys we could ride.

Did I say "ride"? Only three days in the wilderness on horseback and this avowed backpacker, who for years had viewed with disdain all signs of horses in the backcountry, was talking enthusiastically about future horse trips.

I have to admit, however, that the Panther Corners is eminently suited for travel on horse.

Its broad, well drained valleys, low passes and dry, grassy slopes have been traversed by men on horses for decades, with very little impact. The main trail into the area from the east involves several river crossings that would be inconvenient, if not impossible, on foot. From a base camp, most of this vast wilderness can be seen through a series of day trips on horse; on foot several days' provisions would have to be carried in by backpack. Numerous horse camps in the area attest to its popularity for trail-riding in summer and outfitted hunting in fall.

These were the thoughts which coursed through my mind on that warm October night as we raced down the valley blinded by the full harvest moon. The chinook winds pushed at our backs, carrying scents of cured mountain grasses and decaying leaves. At camp, there would be hot food and coffee and rest for weary riding muscles, but I felt I could have ridden forever in this wilderness paradise known as Panther Corners.

Clear, icy water bubbles down in rivulets from the peaks and ridges of the Panther Corners proposed Wildland Recreation Area and disappears in the spongy moss beds under the crowded conifers that line the lower slopes. In the valleys, it reappears, growing in volume as it darts between high, rolling foothills, tumbles over rocky outcrops and weaves through high, open grasslands. The boundaries of the 189 square kilometre proposed Panther Corners Wildland Recreation Area are the Panther, Red Deer and Dormer rivers, and Banff Park.

Popularly known as the "Panther Corners", the area was named for its early reputation as cougar country and for the old park cabin site at the confluence of the Dormer and Panther rivers.

The gentle, open south-facing slopes of the Panther Corners Wildland provide excellent winter range for bighorns and elk, the mainstay of panthers. Relatively remote and unaffected by the human activity near its border, this wilderness provides one of the two most important and extensive elk winter ranges in Alberta.

Frequent chinook winds whisk snow from smooth, high rolling grasslands, exposing the forage needed by the elk for winter food. The most important of these areas, the Ya Ha Tinda grasslands, represents an unusual meeting of prairie and alpine ecosystems.

Just north of the Wildland stretches the Ya Ha Tinda plains, an anomaly in our Rockies, that together with the Panther Corners allows the impressive Dormer elk herd of Banff Park to survive by providing essential winter habitat.

The challenging and scenically diverse Panther Corners was once part of Banff Park, and today provides some of the best fall hunting and summer trail riding opportunities in the province.

Geological History

The area is bounded on the west by the massifs of the front range, Warden's Rock and Barrier Mountain. The broad open slopes of Jap

Mountain dominate the whole wilderness. These mountain masses were pushed upward and eastwards along the Clearwater thrust faults of the front range and the McConnell fault in the east during the Rocky Mountain uplifts. Limestone and dolomite rock up to 500 million years old were sometimes forced over much younger rock. During these geological upheavals, coal-bearing shales some 150-300 million years old came to rest on the top of Jap Mountain.

These coal deposits were formed by the accumulation of vegetation in ancient, swampy deltas. The material was later compressed and compacted into rock. At Panther Dome, just south of the wilderness area, the rock strata were overfolded, trapping deposits of very sour gas which are now of interest to the petroleum industry.

Alpine glaciers were formed at the headwaters of the major river valleys, eroding and widening the valley walls as they moved eastwards. Lobes of ice pushed through Panther Gap, James Pass and Red Deer Gap, first carving base rock, then, as they slowly moved and melted, leaving deposits of sand, silt and gravel in terraces along the flat-bottomed river channels.

Human History

In the past, the Red Deer and Panther river valleys provided access to bountiful hunting grounds. As suggested by more than 50 sites surveyed in the area, native inhabitants camped along main valleys and on the grassy plains north of the Wildland at least 10,000 years ago. These plains, named Ya Ha Tinda or "Little Prairie of the Mountains" by Stoney Indian hunters, today form the federal government's Ya Ha Tinda Ranch where Parks Canada horses are overwintered.

David Thompson, while travelling up the Red Deer River valley to make contact with a band of Kootenay Indians, recorded his impression of the area: "When we arrived near the height of the Mountains, at the foot of these high Crags that have the storm in all its force, I wished to climb them to gain a view of the back country, but they were inaccessible to human feet."

The Panther Corners' value as a wilderness area was recognized as early as 1902 when it was incorporated into the Rocky Mountains Park. The Brewster brothers, famous outfitters and entrepreneurs of the early 1900s, were allowed to lease the Ya Ha Tinda grasslands for horse and cattle grazing, and in 1905 built several log cabins on the prairie for their ranch manager and hired hands. Twelve years later the Brewsters relinquished their land lease, and the Ya Ha Tinda was subsequently used exclusively for the winter grazing of park patrol horses.

A cabin at the confluence of the Dormer and Panther rivers was often used by park rangers and forestry personnel who rode the river valley trails of the national park. It is the site of an existing Forest Service cabin.

With the evolution of Parks Canada policy, along with various boundary changes, the Wildland has twice been part of, and twice excluded from, the park.

In 1971, extensive coal exploration was conducted on the open slopes of Jap Mountain in the heart of the area; the scars of that work will long be visible. However, with the passing of Alberta's Coal Policy in 1976, rugged alpine and subalpine areas including the Panther Corners were declared "off limits" to coal exploration and development.

Exploration for oil and gas has occurred throughout the Panther Corners region. Although a number of exploratory wells were drilled, some as early as the 1950s, none has been drilled within the proposed Wildland Recreation Area.

Wildlife and Vegetation

Chinook winds gust through wide mountain corridors and over the open grasslands of the Wildland. The warming effect of the winds, particularly on the south-facing slopes, encourages the growth of prairie and low elevation plants not usually found in the high country of the Eastern Slopes. Three-flowered avens, dubbed "old man's whiskers" with their feathery leaves, pink-purple flowers and plumed fruit, grow here but are more common in lower grasslands. Rough fescue, a tufted perennial grass favored by grazing animals, grows profusely with June grass on dry south-facing slopes, particularly at the "Corners" and along the upper Red Deer River and Dogrib Creek valley. The only extensive mixed forest occurs on the east side of the Wildland where aspen poplar co-exist with lodgepole pine and spruce trees. The slow growing black spruce, often draped with "old man's beard", occupy some wet, low-lying areas, while subalpine forests are typically of Engelmann spruce, subalpine fir and larch. Moisture-seeking mosses, lichens and woodland flowers grow well in the shade of the subalpine forest. Limber pine stands, uncommon this far north, are found in some portions of the Wildland. Short, twisted limbs on these pines attest to the severity of high altitude environments.

The most hardy of plants occupy the high alpine meadows of the Wildland, providing the nutritious fodder that maintains the extensive herds of wintering wildlife. The open, grassy slopes of the Panther Corners Wildland provide winter forage for as many as 1,000 elk. These elk spend summers in the valleys and meadows of Banff National Park, travelling each fall into the Wildland along the Dormer, Panther and Red Deer River valleys. Elk were transported from Montana to Banff National Park in 1917 and 1919 to replenish the species in Alberta. Elk populations had declined in the late 1800s due to over-hunting, disease and the severe climate. Now the Panther Corners Wildland and the Whaleback in southern Alberta provide perhaps the most important and extensive elk winter ranges in Canada.

Bordering a remote, protected section of Banff National Park, the Panther Corners Wildland is also ideal timber wolf and grizzly bear habitat. Wolves use the entire Wildland as a hunting ground while the grizzly prefers the high country. Grizzlies usually roam the high, open meadows in the western section of the Wildland but have also been seen along Panther Valley, Dormer River and Dogrib Creek. Some grizzlies are also known to winter at Dormer Mountain.

The open south-facing hillsides are a year-around home to many bighorns, and Dogrib Creek is important bighorn sheep and mountain goat territory. The open meadows and woodlands along the Panther and Red Deer valleys provide ample winter range for moose, deer, sheep and even wild horses. Alberta Fish and Wildlife recognizes an area from the Dormer River to the Red Deer River as a critical wildlife habitat and prohibits domestic horse and cattle grazing there.

Recreation

Provincial government studies such as the Foothills Resource Allocation Study, the Recreation Resources Evaluation (Red Deer River Planning Area), and the final draft plan for the Integrated Planning process have recognized the recreation potential of the Red Deer drainage of which Panther Corners is a part. Much of Panther Corners is ideal for family recreation as broad, gentle valleys provide access to subalpine and alpine areas. A number of vehicle access camping sites near the Wildland Recreation Area's borders and a lodge provide ideal staging points for day or extended trips into the wilderness area. Mountainaire Lodge at the junction of the Panther and Red Deer rivers has overnight and dining facilities. A number of trails originate near the lodge and guided canoeing, white water rafting and nordic skiing and horsepacking or day riding tours are conducted from there.

Hunting and Fishing

Each fall the Panther Corners area is visited by elk and sheep hunters, and guided outfitting is a well established and traditional use of the area.

Several lakes are located at high altitudes and some, such as Barrier Lake and Ice Lake, and Eagle Lake outside the Panther Corners Wildland, have been stocked with cutthroat trout. Nearby Dormer Lake is stocked with brook trout. Fishing is a popular pastime in the "Corners". The Panther and Red Deer river systems are open to anglers in alternate years.

An abandoned forestry cabin at the confluence of the Dormer and Panther rivers is often used by trail riders and hikers travelling along the Panther River into Banff National Park. Random campsites abound in the area.

Winter Sports

A number of cross-country skiing and snowshoeing excursions begin at Mountainaire Lodge. The view of the mountains and foothills from the old Dogrib Creek truck trail is impressive but, unfortunately, the trail passes through important deer, elk and moose range which needs protection from heavy winter use.

Water Sports

The white water of the upper Red Deer delights white water enthusiasts each year with its rapids. The river challenges experienced rafters, canoeists and kayakers. Exciting chutes and ledges, opportunities to see wildlife, beautiful scenery and the availability of campsites make this river one of the most popular in southern Alberta for white water sports.

Camping

At vehicle staging areas, there are a number of undeveloped campsites along the Panther River. There also are superb camping areas along elevated flood plains of the upper Red Deer River. These are accessible and scenic and present many opportunities to see moose, elk deer and a variety of waterfowl. Inside the Panther Corners, random horse-based campsites are plentiful, established in the best spots through many years of trail rider and hunter use.

Hiking and Trail Riding

Trails along the Panther and the Dormer rivers can be followed to join major trails in Banff National Park leading to Cascade, Dormer and the upper Red Deer area. A Parks permit must be obtained before entering the national park, however. Some trails in the Panther Corners lead to splendid alpine lakes along the Banff Park boundary, where mountainside basins, scooped out by glaciers, are inviting destinations for those hikers and backpackers and riders seeking a challenge.

Horseback riding is popular along the Panther and Dormer rivers and Dogrib Creek, as well as on the open slopes of Jap Mountain. There are

The picturesque contrast of towering peaks and flowing grasslands at Dogrib Creek in the Panther Corners Wildland.

several small staging areas with corrals along the Panther River outside the Wildland Recreation Area. A horse trail along the easy terrain of Dogrib Valley is heavily used and in need of repair. The historic horse trail up the Panther has largely been replaced by two truck trails, one along the river bed and one high on the north side of the river. Off-road vehicle use of these roads has caused much erosion and conflict with the more traditional uses of the area. To remedy this, the Alberta Forest Service in 1985 designated the Panther Corners as a Forest Land Use Zone, which allows restriction of recreation use of the area, including off-road vehicle use.

Land Use Concerns and Recommendations

All of the Panther Corners Wildland is zoned as Prime Protection under the Eastern Slopes Policy, which means in theory that resource exploration and extraction as well as off-road vehicle use is not permitted. In addition, land near the Ya Ha Tinda Ranch is zoned as Critical Wildlife, which lends additional buffer protection to the area.

Oil, Gas and Coal

Recent events in the Panther Corners clearly illustrate the need for legislation to enforce the Eastern Slopes zoning. In 1982, the Alberta government granted Shell Canada a permit to access the Prime Protection area in the eastern portion of the proposed Panther Corners Wildland. The company built a bridge, road and drilling pad prior to the well application hearing, but withdrew its application before actually drilling, because of new geological information. Similar conflicts can be expected to occur in the future if regulations are not instituted to protect this wilderness area. Although oil and gas exploration is not recommended in Prime Protection Zone lands, "step-out drilling" may be conducted, provided the area to be drilled is part of the same geological structure in which a petroleum company has proven reserves.

A number of oil and gas leases still exist in the area and seven capped wells are located on the southeastern perimeter of Panther Corners. These will probably remain capped until the market suggests they are economical to develop. However, in 1985 one company was testing an old, very sour gas well just south of the "Corners" on Sheep Creek, with a view to producing sulphur. The testing has apparently proved successful, so a major sulphur field could be developed on the very doorstep of the Wildland Recreation Area in the near future.

Jap Mountain was explored for its coal potential in 1971, and coal deposits exist in the area. Fortunately, some reclamation has been done on areas altered by past coal exploration, but many of the exploration scars on the exposed face will never heal.

Logging

There are only a few small tracts of merchantable timber in Panther Corners. Commercial logging is not permitted within these Prime Protection boundaries.

Grazing

With the exception of horse grazing for recreational use, no domestic grazing is permitted within Panther Corners.

Recreational Abuse

Roads near the Wildland Recreation Area's borders, old truck trails, seismic lines and coal exploration roads in the area as well as in the relatively tame eastside landscape all have contributed to the use of off-road vehicles in the area. Some roads such as the Shell access road from the Red Deer and the Jap Mountain coal exploration road have been reclaimed. Lack of regulations to enforce road closures has lead to degradation of most trails and reclamation work in the area.

The 1985 final draft Integrated Resource Plan for the area called for protection through the prohibition of off-road vehicles in the whole Panther Corners. This legislation is presently in effect, although it was instituted with a one-year "sunset clause." It is hoped that citizen support for this protective legislation will ensure its continuation.

In recent years, the use of the Panther Corners by increasing numbers of private and commercial horse parties is leading to some overuse, particularly around alpine lakes and established campsites. Restrictions on horse use under the Forest Land Use Zone legislation are a distinct possibility for the future.

Burnt Timber
Sharp Slope to Gentle Foothills

The short season and the presence of snowmobiles in much of this area mean that the avid cross-country skier must choose his time and place carefully to enjoy the winter solitude of the Burnt Timber Wildland Recreation Area. As with backcountry travel in much of Alberta's Eastern Slopes, the effort is well worth it.

The only maintained access near the area is the Forestry Trunk Road (SR 940), which runs eight to 16 kilometers east of the Wildland Recreation Area. Several of the seismic lines west of the Forestry Trunk Road have been designated by the Alberta Forest Service as snowmobile trails, and during the winter, these machines frequent most of the seismic lines and jeep trails in the area. For these reasons, the skier is usually faced with a fairly long approach before reaching the solitude offered by the isolated portions of the Burnt Timber/Waiparous area.

An excellent way to get a feel for much of the area, and a perfect vantage point for planning future, more ambitious trips, is to ski up the fire road to Mockingbird Hill Lookout. Although the lookout itself, located just north of Waiparous Creek, is outside the proposed Wildland Recreation Area, the view offers glimpses into all its major drainages - Ghost River, Waiparous Creek, Burnt Timber Creek and North Burnt Timber Creek   and a panorama of peaks from Black Rock and Devils Head in the south to Barrier Mountain in the Dormer/Panther country to the north.

The most readily accessible skiing routes are the open valley and stream areas between the Fallen Timber and Waiparous creeks, which include the aptly named Pretty Place Creek. These valleys and drainages offer endless miles of rolling and mostly open skiing terrain which the cross-country enthusiast will share with the numerous moose and wild horses in the area.

The Hunter Valley gas exploration road branches to the west and leads nearly to the headwaters of Burnt Timber Creek. This road provides excellent skiing opportunities, and its termination at 1830 metres makes the ridge on which the Burnt Timber Lookout is located easily accessible. Summer or winter, this ridge offers magnificent views of the Burnt Timber and North Burnt Timber drainages and Banff National Park. This area is also accessible from

A pleasant way to pass the day – casting a line into one of several trout streams in the Burnt Timber Wildland Recreation Area.

On a cloudless day, the view of the Burnt Timber wilderness from the abandoned Blackrock Mountain fire lookout is imposing. Less than two hours from Calgary is a 350 square kilometre wilderness of densely forested valleys, rich alpine meadows, and sheer mountain slopes. The Banff Park boundary has in the past incorporated all or parts of this proposed Wildland Recreation Area, attesting to its beauty and recreation potential.

The wildland beauty of Burnt Timber attracts hikers, hunters, nordic skiers, snowshoers, campers, fishermen, outfitters, climbers and off-road vehicle users.

There is evidence of repeated past fires in the area, and the Burnt Timber Wildland displays various stages of forest regrowth. In some areas, fire has opened forest to grassland, allowing populations of grazing animals such as elk, deer, domestic cattle and feral horses to flourish. Bighorn sheep and mountain goats also flourish, occupying higher reaches along the front ranges overlooking the Burnt Timber foothills. Moose are also a common species.

This wilderness is vulnerable to abuse. Increasing recreational vehicle activity, exploratory sour gas drilling and the introduction of seismic lines and exploration roads threaten the wilderness and wildlife of the Burnt Timber.

Like the South Ghost proposed Wildland Recreation Area, the Burnt Timber was a place of mystery and awe to the Indians who frequently hunted in this area. Tomahawks have been found by visitors, and religious ceremonies are believed to have been conducted at Devils Head Mountain.

This wilderness deserves absolute protection

the north via Panther River and Sheep Creek, although deep snow may make for a long ski approach to the North Burnt Timber drainage.

The area known locally as "Sheep Crest" at the extreme eastern edge of the front ranges, just north of Waiparous Creek, is probably the most inviting terrain for those interested in ski mountaineering. The slopes of the "Crest" hold snow well into the spring and offer a variety of enjoyable slopes for skiers of all abilities.

Despite its accessibility from Calgary and a reasonable snow cover for three to four months a year, none of the Burnt Timber/Waiparous area is frequented by skiers. This in large part is due to the predominance, in summer as well as winter, of motorized recreation activity in this area. The fact that such activity drives out non-motorized recreation is an additional argument for setting aside these highly scenic and accessible lands as a Wildland Recreation Area.

because of its potential for wildlife and recreation. Scenic and close to settlement, the Burnt Timber can provide quality wilderness experiences that are becoming increasingly rare in the populated southern part of the province.

Geological History

The Burnt Timber area, like much of the Eastern Slopes, reveals today the passage of many eras. It was once an ocean bottom, once a tropical forest, and was once covered by a massive sheet of ice. Its sedimentary rock reveals its varied past: in the prolific and watery world that existed between 570 and 65 million years ago, layer upon layer of compressed life accumulated on the bottom of deep, quiet sea beds which are today the thick, fossil-bearing limestone and dolomite rock common in the area. The shale and loose, sandy rock were formed while the waters receded, and the region was characterized by shallow lakes, bays and lagoons. Over a period of 500 million years, sediments of the Cambrian and Tertiary eras accumulated to depths of thousands of metres, then compacted and hardened over time.

The undisturbed sedimentary rock-building process ended about 65 million years ago, when subterranian disturbances began pushing buried rock up and over the existing formations. The abrupt rise of the east side of the Rockies is the result of the easterly thrust of the Rocky Mountain front ranges during this time, but the landscape we see today was etched by erosion, glacier movement and weathering.

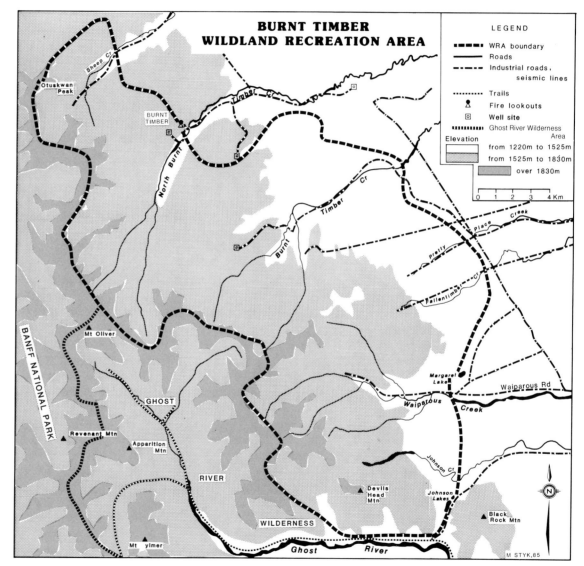

Glaciers from the great alpine ice caps of the Rockies carved the landscapes of the Burnt Timber region until about 10,000 years ago. Evidence from glacial deposits shows that the *ice may have been about 600 metres thick,* and only the tops of the highest peaks could have protruded through the frozen sea. These glaciers, which originated in the high alpine areas, moved eastwards as great tongues of ice along the valleys of Devil's Gap and the Red Deer, Bow and Ghost rivers. The moving ice gouged the U-shaped valleys of North Burnt Timber Creek and left steep-walled rock basins or cirques in the mountains. As the glaciers retreated and melted, torrents of water, sand, gravel and mud were washed down in the streams in the region, depositing extensive gravel outwash plains along major streams in the area, a feature distinctive today.

Human History

"Cold, bare and rugged crags, almost perpendicular. The demon of the mountains alone could fix his dwelling there." So said one of the first white men to visit the Burnt Timber area, George Simpson, Governor-in-Chief of the Hudson's Bay Company. Simpson travelled along the Red Deer River on a Stoney Indian trail, entering the mountains via Devil's Gap in the mid-1800s.

Simpson's description of the region's crags as a demon's home was apt. Devils Head Mountain in the Wildland Recreation Area acquired its name because its pinnacle of rock

bore a rough resemblance to a sinister, upturned face. Artifacts found on the mountain indicate the landform may have been of religious significance to the Indians. Apparently they believed that the spirits of warriors slain in battles between Stoney and Blackfoot tribes lingered along the nearby Ghost River, formerly called Dead Man's River.

In the late 1800s, the horns of trophy rams were prized commodities among white men. The Stoneys often hunted these animals in the Burnt Timber Wildland, bringing their trade goods into the Canmore corridor.

The new transcontinental railroad built through the Bow corridor in the late 1800s brought a few hardy settlers to the area. By the turn of the century, the McDougalls, the first family to settle in the Burnt Timber, had established Devils Head Ranch on the eastern border of the area. The McDougalls relinquished the land when it became part of the protected Rocky Mountain Forest Reserve just after the turn of the century. The property was later removed from the reserve and purchased by the Brewster family as winter range for dude horses used in Banff Park during the tourist season. The Brewster cabin, built in 1926 at Meadow Creek southeast of the Wildland Recreation Area, is still inhabited and in good condition.

Devils Head Mountain lured several curious climbers to its summit in early years. A Philadelphia climber, Samuel Allen, reached the peak in 1891. Thirty-four years later, two original members of the Alpine Club of Canada, Louis Crosby and Dr. J. Hickson, climbed the Devils Head. Hickson, a writer, philosopher and avid mountaineer, had been the first man on 30 peaks in the Rockies and Alps, most of which are more

than 3000 metres high. Other early recreational uses of the Burnt Timber included hunting and outfitting trips conducted by Indians and local outfitters like the Brewsters.

Ranchers drove cattle, horses and domestic sheep into the Burnt Timber's grassy meadows for grazing. Logging companies harvested the Burnt Timber and Fallen Timber creeks as well as the Ghost and Waiparous basins east of the proposed Wildland Recreation Area. Logs were floated down the Ghost and Bow rivers to Calgary sawmills.

To protect timber resources from fire, in 1927 the Alberta government constructed a fire lookout on Blackrock Mountain at the southeast corner of the Burnt Timber Wildland. The post was abandoned in 1963.

In the 1950s, the scramble to tap Alberta's oil and gas potential reached the wilderness of the Burnt Timber. The era is marked in the Burnt Timber by seismic cutlines which criss-cross the region's forests. Today there are several new "step-out" wells in the Wildland's northern portion as well as new well access roads. A good deal of reclamation work on abandoned exploration roads has recently been carried out by the petroleum industry.

Wildlife and Vegetation

For the keen photographer, hiker and naturalist, the Burnt Timber offers many opportunities to view wildlife amidst a variety of habitats.

In poorly drained areas along valley bottoms, wet meadows of sedge, willow and bog birch carpet the ground and maintain a healthy population of moose. Moose, elk and deer are often seen along Burnt Timber drainages. Gravel streambeds, common in the area, are dotted with yellow dryads and shaded by moisture-seeking trees like spruce, poplar and aspen poplar. Seeds, leaves and berries provide summer feeding for the ruffed and spruce grouse. Willow and poplar buds provide winter food. Beaver dams back up water on small creeks, forming ponds and marshes. The lowlands of the Burnt Timber Wildland host coyote, mink, blackbear, weasel, fisher and lynx, though populations have decreased with the heavy use of the region by off-road vehicles.

The vegetation of many parts of the Burnt Timber, as its name implies, has been influenced by fire. Forest cleared by fire provides grazing land for mule deer and elk. Several herds of feral horses in the area also compete with elk and cattle for forage.

At subalpine elevations, the dark, dense forests of Engelmann spruce and alpine fir shelter mosses and lichens, the delicate pink twin-flower, fragrant wintergreen, the leathery-leaved bog cranberry and the spectacular and elusive Calypso orchid.

Tree growth tapers off at the alpine zone. Although stunted trees may occasionally be found, herbs and lichens are generally the only growth which can withstand the short growing season, high winds and soil conditions. Alpine plants have adapted to this environment. The snow willow, for instance, grows close to the ground or in sheltered rock crevices. White mountain avens capture water in their leaf hairs, while the rose-root stores water in its fleshy stem and leaves. Other common flowering plants include golden fleabane, a tiny perennial with

disproportionately large yellow flowers, as well as Indian paintbrush and goldenrod.

The high, open country of this zone, particularly along the front range in the proposed area, is favored by both grizzly and black bears. Hikers should be especially cautious on slopes, in heavily vegetated areas, near thick deadfall where visibility is limited and near noisy streams. Winter range for bighorn sheep and mountain goats is on the headwaters of the North and South Burnt Timber creeks. Their summer range is all along the exposed front range and into the adjacent national park lands.

Recreation

There are a number of Alberta Forest Service campsites along the Trunk Road to the east and northwest of the Wildland Recreation Area. These campsites are excellent points from which to launch trips into the Burnt Timber. Recently, the Waiparous River has become a popular place for organized group camps, especially church camps.

Johnson Creek meadow, nestled in a broad, picturesque valley to the east of Burnt Timber Wildland, is a favoured recreation area. Johnson Lakes on the Burnt Timber's eastern border attract fishermen, while Devils Head meadow, between the truck trail and Johnson Creek, provides a superb view of the Rockies. There is random camping throughout parts of this wilderness, particularly along the North Burnt Timber Creek and Waiparous Creek. The upper Waiparous Creek area, with its broad valleys,

forested slopes and steep cliffs, attracts campers seeking solitude. However, the lower reaches of this valley west of the Forestry Trunk Road are part of the Ghost River recreational vehicle area.

Hiking, Trail Riding, Climbing

Trail riding has great potential in the North Burnt Timber valley and its headwaters as well as along Pinto Creek. A number of commercial outfitters have base camps to the southeast of the Wildland Recreation Area and frequently run day-long trail rides into the area. Devils Head meadow is an especially beautiful riding area.

Hikers can use existing game trails and seismic lines, especially at high elevations in the West Burnt Timber region. Some trails, such as those along the Ghost River, can be travelled into the Ghost River Wilderness Area and on into Banff National Park. Cross-country routes lead over rugged passes into Banff Park. A permit is needed to enter the park for overnight visits. The upper Waiparous is especially rugged, with many beautiful water-carved pools and waterfalls.

Hunting and Fishing

Bull trout, closely related to Arctic char, are native to Burnt Timber, Pinto and the North Burnt Timber creeks. Increased motorized access into these areas has resulted in overfishing of this species. As a result, Pinto Creek has been closed until the fish population recovers. Fortunately,

many creeks in the Wildland have been stocked with cutthroat trout, a more resilient fish than bull trout.

Rainbow trout can be found in the fast waters of the North Burnt Timber Creek's south fork. Eastern brook trout are common in streams with beaver impoundments. Rocky Mountain whitefish, one of the most common game fish in Alberta, are found downstream of the falls in the central reaches of North Burnt Timber Creek. The Burnt Timber water system is closed in alternate years to allow recovery of fish populations. In contrast to the Burnt Timber drainage, the Waiparous drainage has limited fish habitat because of the lack of quiet pools.

A small number of trophy bighorn rams are taken from this area, as well as an occasional grizzly. Hunting seasons for mountain goats have been closed since 1969. Moose, deer and grouse are the main species hunted. Elk occur in this wilderness but their numbers have been reduced by habitat change and past hunting pressures. They also bear the brunt of competition for food from cattle and feral horses.

Winter Sports

Chinooks and exposure to the sun in open valleys makes snow cover unpredictable for winter sports in southern parts of the Wildland Recreation Area. There is more snow and less effect from chinooks in the north, and the potential there for non-motorized winter recreation such as cross-country skiing is high.

FACING PAGE: *Remnants of a forest fire in the headwaters of the Burnt Timber.*

Land Use Concerns and Recommendations

Oil, Gas and Coal

Much of the Burnt Timber is zoned Prime Protection or Critical Wildlife Habitat, which prohibits or restricts the exploration for or extraction of minerals. Still, a few test wells have been drilled outside the Burnt Timber and several new wells and their attendant roads have recently been drilled on Prime Protection lands within the proposed Wildland Recreation Area, under the "step out" program.

Coal deposits in the area exist along Sheep Creek in the northwest corner. Under the Alberta Coal Policy, however, there is no coal exploration or development permitted in the Burnt Timber Wildland.

The predominant threat to the Burnt Timber wilderness lands is the use of off-road vehicles, which destroy vegetation, disturb wildlife and depreciate the area's potential for other recreation uses. Gentle terrain on the east side of the proposed Wildland Recreation Area, easy access to roads and seismic lines, and a nearby area designated for off-highway vehicle use compound the problem.

Grazing

Although the entire Burnt Timber unit is under grazing permit, competition for forage between cattle and wildlife is not a threat at this time. Serious overgrazing and trampling of stream beds by cattle has in the past led to a recommendation that use of valley bottoms and stream beds for domestic grazing be forbidden throughout the important Ghost drainage district. Feral horses, however, may need to be controlled to eliminate terrain damage and competition with wildlife.

Forestry

A Sundre logging company has held an active licence in the Burnt Timber for many years. The company has not yet logged in the area, although it may wish to renew its licence in 1986. Past forest fires in the region have left timber too immature to harvest at present. If logging is conducted in the near future, it will likely be in the upper Fallentimber Creek area near the border of the Wildland Recreation Area proposal. In order to maintain viable wildlife populations, the natural cycle of fires will perhaps need to be encouraged through controlled burning.

Recommendations

This wildland deserves protection because of its value for wildlife and wildland recreation. It is a crucial buffer zone between developed landscapes to the east and the Ghost Wilderness and Banff National Park to the west. There are 37 kilometres of industrial roads and seismic lines which have not yet been reclaimed or closed to motor vehicle access. The closure of these roads which run through fragile areas would still leave some 500 kilometres of roads and seismic lines open to off-road vehicles between the Ghost River and the North Burnt Timber, west of the Forestry Trunk Road, outside the proposed Wildland Recreation Area.

South Ghost
A Rugged Beauty

Cross-country skiing opportunities in the South Ghost Wildland Recreation Area are usually restricted to the South Ghost River drainage, although in years of heavy snowfall the more rugged canyons of Cougar Creek and Exshaw Creek in the south and the open headwater areas of Old Fort Creek in the southeast of the area also provide feasible snowshoeing and cross-country ski routes. The exposed ridges of the area and the higher south and west slopes tend to blow free of snow, resulting in poor skiing conditions but also making available winter range for the mountain goat and sheep populations in the area.

Depending on the seasonal snow pack, a skier travelling into the South Ghost River drainage may start as far east as the Bar Cee Ranch at 1370 metres elevation on the Forestry Trunk Road (SR 940) in a heavy snowfall year or, more commonly, at the mouth of the South Ghost canyon between End Mountain and Orient Peak at approximately 1670 metres. The incidence of chinook winds in this area and the cobbled nature of the river valley tend to restrict the ski season to December, January and February.

On the lower slopes of the south and southeast sides of Orient Point, above the former site of "Hussey's cabin" on the river, ambitious skiers may practice their telemarking and other skiing manoeuvres within sight of the bighorn sheep on their winter range.

If the skier decides to continue the gradual climb up the canyon of the South Ghost from this point, each turn in the river bed will reveal a further glimpse of the heart of this area. Falling away from Saddle Peak on the north side of the canyon is an imposing but miniature version of Devils Head Peak - its geological "big brother" rising above the Ghost River two valleys to the north. The seismic line running diagonally up the river bed gradually disappears altogether near the 1890 metre elevation. Here the canyon splits and the serious climbing begins.

Broad open slopes and deep-drifted snow can be found throughout the headwaters of the Ghost and its minor tributaries from the north. Either dense forest or steep avalanche-prone slopes must be traversed to reach these. Skiers should therefore be wary of avalanche hazard conditions. Above 1890 metres and even further down the valley behind you your tracks may be the only ones of the season in this seldom visited area.

As in much of the Eastern Slopes readily accessible to large populations, snowmobile users do travel into this area in the winter. It appears to be less popular, however, than the valleys immediately to the north and these vehicles find the terrain in the canyon very rugged once the 1830 metre elevation is reached.

Many Calgarians and out-of-town visitors have sped by the proposed South Ghost Wildland on their way to Banff and points west. On a clear day, the Wildland's ragged peaks can be seen from Calgary, about 70 kilometres away. The Trans-Canada Highway skirts the Wildland's southern border, while to its northwest is Lake Minnewanka, a busy camping, hiking, boating and fishing destination in Banff National Park. The Wildland's eastern border abuts the Stoney Indian Reserve, and its western boundary is shared with Banff Park.

Remarkably, this 240 square kilometre unit, so close to major thoroughfares and recreational developments, is one of the most untamed and pristine regions of Alberta's Eastern Slopes.

Visitors to the area are rarely troubled by off-road vehicles and can still reach grassy alpine meadows seen primarily by bighorn sheep and mountain goats. Here, strong winds chase clouds over barren peaks and tug grasses from their shallow footholds in thin alpine soil. This land inspires us, not with its beauty, but with its rawness and magnificence. It also teases the

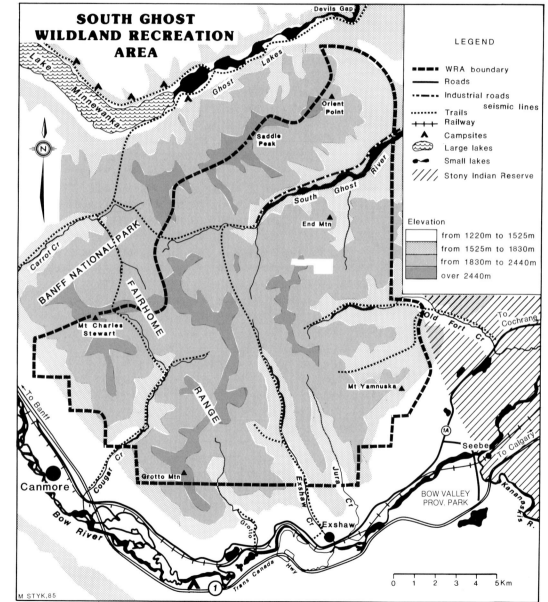

imagination, with its tales of the Ghost or Dead Man's River, Devils Head Mountain and a haunted cabin.

Several outfitters based near the Wildland guide hunting and riding parties into the region. Since the rugged terrain has discouraged large-scale resource exploration, there is little to detract from the natural splendour of the land. Its high cliffs and towering peaks provide buffers between natural regions like the Ghost Wilderness Area and Banff National Park, and settled areas to the south and southeast.

With a major highway at its doorstep and several Alberta Forest Service Campsites near its border, the South Ghost offers ideal staging points for extended trips into the wilds. The South Ghost is accessible by a seasonal road running west from the North Forestry Road off Highway 1A.

This area's recreational potential and wild character, its value as a watershed and important sheep and goat range, and its proximity to Calgary make the South Ghost an ideal candidate for wildland preservation.

Geological History

About 65 million years ago, a major fault in the South Ghost region slipped, thrusting old, previously buried rock eastward over younger sandstone formations. From this, the McConnell thrust fault emerged, an impressive mountain range which exposed 600-million-year-old Cambrian rock, 450-million-year-old Mississippian sedimentary rock, and 130-million-year-old Cretaceous rock. These formations are exposed in limestone and dolomite cliffs, some of which rise to more than 900 metres along the east side of the Wildland.

Steep cliffs also guard the South Ghost River, a section of which descends quickly from glaciated ridges and drops 300 metres in just four kilometres. Spring runoff into the South Ghost River seeps underground, flowing through porous limestone bedrock. By mid-summer, the lower 16 kilometres of the river dries up, earning its name Dry Fork.

Human History

The Bow Valley along the southern boundary of the Wildland was an important transportation route for explorers, Indians, fur traders and settlers. Although the adventurers frequently passed the South Ghost, there was little reason to travel through its rugged backcountry. As a result, most historical events occurred near, but seldom in, the area.

The Hudson's Bay Company in 1832 built a trading post just east of the proposed Wildland to lure Peigan and Blackfoot Indians away from American traders on the Missouri. The Old Bow Fort or Peigan Post, as it was called, raised the wrath of the Peigan Indians. Barred from using the new post, angry Peigans harassed trading parties until the post was abandoned just two years after its construction.

In 1857 botanist Eugene Bourgeau and geologist Dr. James Hector of the Palliser expedition discovered a mountainside cave in the Wildland, and named the mountain Grotto Mountain. Pigeon and Wind mountains, south of the Wildland, were also aptly named by these explorers during their attempts to describe and map the region.

The Trans-Continental Railway, completed in 1883 through the Bow Corridor, welcomed early visitors including hunters, trail riders, mountain climbers and sightseers. Trophy ram hunting became popular in the 1900s, although the Stoney Indians had long since discovered the region's hunting potential. Fred Hussey, a wealthy Pittsburgh man who hunted in the area, built a cabin at the headwaters of the South Ghost River in 1929. A partner in Pittsburgh Steel and Brewster Outfitting, Hussey used the cabin for several years, then abandoned it. Local ranchers and hunters used and maintained the cabin until it burned down in 1977 or 1978. Some claim it was haunted. The Stoneys were apparently wary of the site although there are no recorded tales of tragedy or horror around which the legend was built.

Local Indians were also wary of the Ghost River or Dead Man's River. The slain of battles between the Stoney and the Blackfoot tribes were buried on a hill overlooking the river, and the area was believed to hold mystical and religious significance.

Wildlife and Vegetation

Wind and a severe climate limit vegetation growth in this high, rock-stewn wild country. Summer winds lift thin, poorly anchored soil and

Tucked away from the hustle and bustle of the nearby TransCanada Highway, upper Exshaw Creek reaches out its tranquil hand.

Recreation

Outfitters, hikers and students of many organizations use the Wildland regularly. Staging points near the South Ghost include parking areas and campgrounds along Highway 1A, and campgrounds near Lake Minnewanka in Banff Park. Highway access to the area is excellent.

Most trails are steep. There is a good, less-steep path used by locals and hikers along the South Ghost drainage. Grotto Creek Trail is an interesting hike. The trail follows scenic streams and winds through a narrow gorge, converging with other creeks in a valley. The trail continues on to one of several caves in the area which have been formed by underground streams. Indian pictographs have been seen on some of the cave walls in the Wildland Recreation Area.

Land Use Concerns and Recommendations

Rugged, barren and majestic, the South Ghost should be protected. The Alberta Wilderness Association (AWA) supports the recommendation made in an Alberta government study on the park potential of the Eastern Slopes: "The South Ghost unit is suited to rugged wilderness hiking. It should be designated for wildland recreation."

The AWA also recommends that one seismic line extending about 6.5 kilometres up the South Ghost River which intrudes into critical wildlife habitat be reclaimed as soon as possible.

vegetation. Chinook winds in winter drift and melt the snow, exposing vegetation to the harsh elements. Because of the wind and its effects, few of the common Eastern Slopes animal species like moose, elk, deer and blackbear inhabit South Ghost Wildland, as it lacks suitable low-elevation habitat. As a result, the wildlife and fisheries resources are limited in this primarily alpine and subalpine region.

The alpine zone has sedge meadows and grasses which provide winter and summer forage for sheep and goats. Pikas and ground squirrels are also common. Subalpine forests are of sparse Engelmann spruce, lodgepole pine, alpine fir, alpine larch and in northern areas, whitebark pine. The South Ghost valley is characterized by pine and mature spruce. Meadows of grass and shrubs punctuate pine-covered slopes, the more lush of these providing forage for sheep and goats.

Elbow/Sheep
The Wilderness Next Door

The Upper Elbow/Sheep provides a surprising variety of backpacking possibilities within an hour's drive of Calgary. It never fails to amaze me that this long, narrow Wildland Recreation Area, which can be easily crossed in one day, has so many interesting multi-day trips within its boundaries. It is especially suited to early and late season hiking when there is too much snow in the higher parts of the Rockies.

Major access corridors into the Upper Elbow/Sheep include the Elbow River and Little Elbow River valleys from the Ford Creek campground on Highway 66; the Sheep River valley from the Bluerock campground on Highway 546; and the Evans-Thomas Creek, Elbow Lake and Mist Creek valleys from Highway 40.

Running shoes are the footware of choice for hiking in many of the main valleys of the region, since you will be walking on hard gravel roads that are now closed to motorized traffic. Running shoes will also speed things up at the generally easy fords that you will encounter, especially on the Sheep River.

Most of the popular hikes in the Upper Elbow/Sheep are described in the *Kananaskis Country Trail Guide*, an indispensable reference for those who plan to backpack in the area. An article in the July/August 1983 issue of *Explore* magazine describes the proposed Foothills Wilderness Trail, a four to six day trip that follows the eastern edge of the Upper Elbow/Sheep. Alberta Recreation and Parks produces trail maps of the Elbow and Sheep valleys.

The key to enjoying the Upper Elbow/Sheep, however, is not to limit yourself to the major valley bottoms or the guide book routes. Because the Elbow/Sheep is a relatively dry area, the forests are usually quite open and bushwhacking is never very difficult. A topographic map is all you will need to discover interesting side valleys and breathtaking ridge walks.

The proposed Elbow/Sheep Wildland Recreation Area is in the heart of Kananaskis Country, just 40 kilometres southwest of Calgary. It is flanked at its western border by Highway 40 and at its eastern border by popular foothills recreation areas of the lower Elbow and Sheep valleys. The busy Trans-Canada Highway is to the immediate north. Surrounding these wilderness lands are

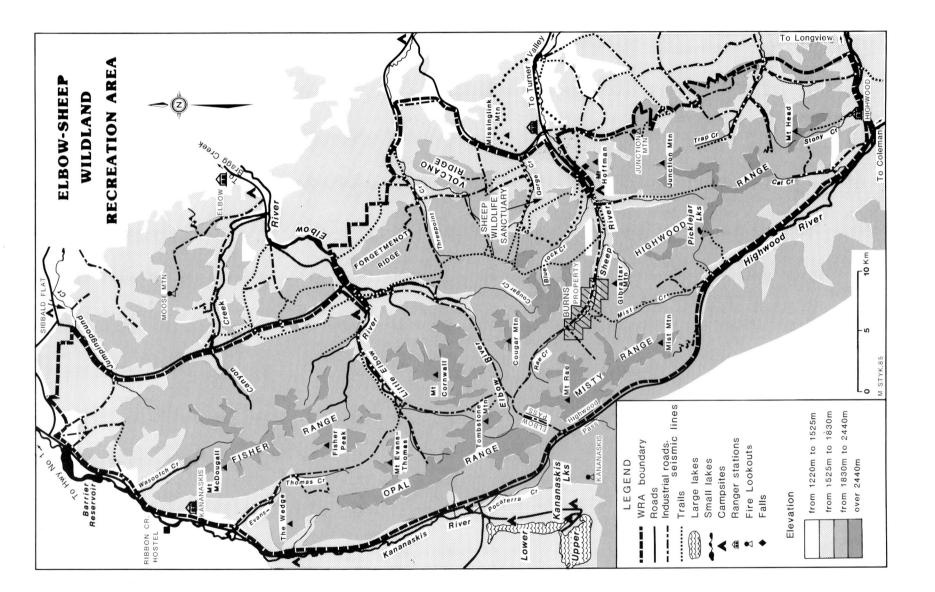

ELBOW-SHEEP
WILDLAND
RECREATION AREA

LEGEND

WRA boundary
Roads
Industrial roads,
seismic lines
Trails
Large lakes
Small lakes
Campsites
Ranger stations
Fire Lookouts
Falls

Elevation

from 1220m to 1525m
from 1525m to 1830m
from 1830m to 2440m
over 2440m

0   5   10 Km

M. STYK. 85

A view into the unmarred headwaters of the Elbow and Sheep rivers. This Wildland Recreation Area, an hour's drive from Calgary, is a rugged wilderness with a wide variety of scenery and terrain.

golfing, downhill skiing, camping, motor touring and all-terrain vehicle destinations.

In spite of the activity at its borders, the Elbow/Sheep remains a rugged and serene wilderness of front range mountains and foothills. About 70 percent of its landscape is above 1830 metres, historically providing natural barriers to human manipulation. Larger than Yoho National Park at 1440 square kilometres, the Elbow/Sheep presents an opportunity few other areas of the world offer: the opportunity of maintaining a wilderness complete with an array of mountain wildlife next door to a major city.

Indian nations once vied for hunting territory in the Elbow/Sheep's grasslands and forests. Ranchers later found the rich meadows in its foothills for grazing their cattle. Early on, its natural beauty, wildlife and fish became cherished favourites for many of the nearby growing communities.

Not only does the area today continue to provide the untrammelled settings sought by increasing numbers of outdoor enthusiasts, it provides most of the water for their homes. The area gives rise to the headwaters of the Elbow and Sheep rivers, which provide 19 percent of the water in the entire Bow River system. The Elbow is the major water source for the city of Calgary.

Often taken for granted in the past when most of western Canada was wilderness, the scarcity of wilderness today and the pressures of a growing nearby population have turned attention toward protecting the Elbow/Sheep, the irreplaceable wilderness next door.

Although coal seams and oil and gas reserves underlie a substantial portion of the Wildland, the Elbow/Sheep's rugged terrain has inhibited the development of these resources. Most of the area is zoned Prime Protection or Critical Wildlife, where development of non-renewable resources is not recommended. Today, the area appears almost as flawless as it did when Indian hunters first travelled its long valleys.

Important bighorn sheep and mountain goat ranges lie within the Wildland, and a wildlife sanctuary on the eastern border of the Elbow/Sheep helps to preserve bighorn sheep populations. The Elbow/Sheep also boasts some 244 bird species, among them the slate-blue harlequin duck (a maritime species) and the rare pileated woodpecker. A variety of plants, some rare in Alberta, contribute to the diversity of life in the proposed Wildland Recreation Area.

Recreation opportunities abound. Visitors can enjoy hiking, camping, hunting and fishing, climbing, nature appreciation, canoeing and horse packing within the Wildland's borders.

Geological History

The Elbow/Sheep wilderness contains both the foothills physiographic unit in the eastern portion of the proposed Wildland Recreation Area and the much more complex folded front ranges of the Rocky Mountains on its west side.

Ten to 20 million years ago, massive fault blocks of Paleozoic limestones, dolomites and quartzite were thrust eastward over the younger Mesozoic strata of the foothills to form the northeast-southwest-trending Opal, Misty, Fisher and Highwood mountain ranges. Movement along these thrust faults ranged from several hundred metres to many kilometres.

In addition to thrust faults, other features associated with mountain building such as anticlines and synclines are repeated eastward through the mountain section of the Elbow/Sheep. On the east side of the Opal and Misty ranges, a syncline occupied by the upper part of the Highwood valley and Mist Creek extends northward as far as the headwaters of the Little Elbow. Mesozoic shales and sandstones occur along the syncline. In the vicinity of Rickerts Pass on the sharp divide between Mist Creek and the Sheep River, the coal-bearing Kootenay formation was brought to the surface. Here, the coal seams range in thickness from one to six metres.

Many of the large cliff faces seen in these mountains are formed from erosion-resistant carbonate rocks of the Mississipian and Devonian ages. Weathering has created spectacular rugged scenery, with the towering cliffs of Mount Gibralter and unnamed peaks in the Opal Range being notable examples.

An anticline runs north-south between Mount Romulus and Mount Remus. The east limb of this anticline becomes the west limb of the syncline running through Compression Ridge, Nihahi Ridge and along the eastern slope of Mount Glasgow. This syncline is faulted on the eastward side for its entire length, effectively marking the east boundary of the mountains.

The folding and faulting is much less complex in the foothills. The foothills are underlain by the relatively more erodable Mesozoic sandstones and shales, resulting in gentle landscapes. The higher hills are capped with more resistant sandstone, while the valleys consist mainly of soft, easily weathered shales. The underground disappearance of some streams in the area can be explained by the presence of glacially deposited gravel beds, and perhaps by some surface faulting.

In addition to these deposits, glaciation has left its mark in the formation of numerous cirques, hanging valleys, U-shaped valleys and stream terraces. It is believed that a stream at one time flowed through the present Elbow Pass and down the Elbow River, but the area west of the Pass was later captured by development of Pocaterra Creek, and only the continuous valley itself now remains as evidence.

Human History

With its abundance of elk, bighorn sheep, deer and bison, the valleys and grassy slopes of the Elbow/Sheep were popular and often disputed hunting grounds for the Stoney, Peigan and Kootenay Indians.

Bordering the wilderness lands of the Elbow/Sheep were two ancient north-south trails which were used extensively by the Kootenay and Stoney peoples. As well, there were east-west trail links through the Rockies making use of such routes as Elbow Pass. The route of one of the main north-south trails lay along the Kananaskis River and the Highwood River, making use of the Highwood Pass between Pocaterra Creek and Storm Creek. Though a rough route, the mountain seclusion of the trail afforded some safety for the Kootenay and Stoney from their Blackfoot enemies of the prairies. Today, this ancient route is Highway 40 and the western boundary to the proposed Wildland Recreation Area.

Though less safe, a much easier route to travel, known as the Stoney Trail, lay along the east slope of the Rockies from Rocky Mountain House to Waterton Lakes. This trail crossed the Elbow River about 16 kilometres downstream of the present Elbow ranger station. This trail was used by pioneers, including the McDougalls, who were early missionaries to the Stoneys, as the main route between the North Saskatchewan and Montana until the eastern prairie route became safer in later years.

Invariably, clashes took place between the Kootenays, Stoneys, and Blackfoot, as each considered the other an intruder to their territory. There is an account of a raid around 1855 by the Blackfoot on a Stoney camp just south of Sheep River on the west bank of a deep coulee not far from Sheep River ranger station. Two of the Stoney men went hunting early one morning while the other three remained in camp to take a sweat bath. A party of Blackfoot surprised the camp, and the women and children fled west along the banks of the Sheep River until they were able to gain the seclusion of timber. The Stoney bathers had time only to don their moccasins, shirts and belts before the attack began. One old woman, a sister of Chief David Bearspaw, remained with the three men and aided them by carrying a sack of shot right into the skirmish. When the shot bag was almost empty, the old woman picked up an axe, and danced and sang a powerful medicine song. At that moment, a cloudburst occurred which drenched the Blackfoot and dampened their powder. The Stoneys on the west bank remained dry and kept sniping at the confused enemy. The Stoney men bravely held off the attackers and miraculously escaped without being wounded, at the same time having taken a heavy toll of the Blackfoot. The old woman had demonstrated the fearsome powers of her people in bringing the mountain storm to their assistance, so the Blackfoot withdrew, leaving their dead in the coulee. Hastily, the Stoneys broke camp, gathered their horses and families and moved towards the headwaters of Sheep River where they felt sure the Blackfoot would not follow.

Today, a very important archeological site at Sibbald Flats in the northeast corner of the Elbow/Sheep is a Provincial Historic Reserve.

A very early group of western settlers in 1854 made their way through the area. One hundred and twenty-one pioneers of the Red River settlement under the leadership of James Sinclair travelled up the Kananaskis along the western boundary of the proposed Wildland Recreation Area en route to British Columbia. This perilous journey was part of a plan to reinforce British claims to the disputed Oregon Territory by

bringing settlers into present-day southern British Columbia. Their Indian guide planned to take the 23 families along a supposedly easier and shorter route than Whiteman Pass, but he became lost in the tangle of deadfall. The treachery of mountain trails choked with deadfall from recent fires forced them to abandon their Red River carts. The pass they actually crossed is uncertain, being either the North Kananaskis Pass or one of the Elk Passes. The Palliser Expedition four years later reported finding some abandoned ox carts along the Kananaskis River. Much later, in 1939, remains of ox carts were reported near the mouth of Evans/Thomas Creek. Could these have been the Red River carts of 1854?

Both Sinclair and Captain John Palliser found the whole country of Kananaskis Valley ravaged by fire. Several gold prospectors soon followed Palliser's footsteps into the Elbow/Sheep region, but the area was never esteemed for its potential for gold, at least not by non-believers in the folklore of the Lost Lemon Mine.

According to local folklore, a character named Blackjack, apparently a pioneer of the Caribou gold rush, and his partner Lemon, from Montana, were following an old Indian trail along the Eastern Slopes of southern Alberta in the 1860s when they accidentally discovered gold. Predictably, an argument over the gold ensued. While Blackjack was sleeping, his partner murdered him with an axe and fled. Two Stoneys who had witnessed the event returned to their reserve at Morleyville to tell Chief Bearspaw. The chief insisted on keeping the story a secret in order to save their hunting grounds from gold prospectors, and decreed that a curse would befall anyone involved with the gold.

Meanwhile, insane with guilt, Lemon confessed to a priest, who sent John McDougall to bury Blackjack's body. McDougall is said to have piled stones over the corpse but Bearspaw's braves returned later to obliterate all evidence of the grave and the crime. Although many people have searched the headwaters of the Highwood and the Livingstone Range area for signs of the camp or the gold, it has never been found. Skeptics believe the tale was fabricated in the 1860s to encourage people to finance prospecting parties.

In 1884, Dr. G.W. Dawson, working for the Geological Survey of Canada, described the Elbow/Sheep lands and gave English names to many of their features. Misty Range and Storm Mountain were named for surrounding weather conditions. Tombstone Mountain was named for the collection of pinnacle-like slabs near its summit, and the Opal Range for its small cavities lined with quartz crystals coated with an opal film. Mount Rae, the highest peak in the Elbow/Sheep, had already been named by Sir James Hector during his 1858-59 expeditions.

At the turn of the century, the buffalo were gone and ranchers were discovering the grazing meadows of the Elbow/Sheep. The Stoneys were forced to move further west in search of game but were restricted by territorial conflicts with the Kootenays. Domestic livestock were moved into the area, often overgrazing areas which provided important sources of forage for wild game. Each spring, cowboys from such famous pioneer ranches as the Bar U and the Buffalo Head herded cattle into lush valleys in the eastern portion of the Elbow/Sheep Wildland for summer grazing. Choice river bottoms of the Highwood and Sheep rivers were favorite ranges.

The period around the turn of the century also brought demands for coal, timber and oil and gas, which lead some people to the Elbow/Sheep. By 1896, Dawson's report "The Country in the Vicinity of the Bow and Belly Rivers [today's Oldman, Crowsnest and Castle rivers], Northwest Territories" was being used extensively by private citizens and exploration companies to investigate the Elbow/Sheep's potential. Timber births in the region were set by 1884 to allow logging of those accessible stands that had escaped earlier extensive fires.

Settlers often mined the black coal seam outcroppings of the area for personal fuel. A promising coal deposit was located on the upper reaches of the Sheep River in the central portion of the Elbow/Sheep Wildland. Pat Burns, an affluent Calgary businessman later to become a senator, purchased 4000 hectares of this land. A railway grade was built, a power plant was constructed and the coal mine began operations. However, the advent of the First World War and a corresponding decline in the coal market left the ambitious plans for the Burns Mine unfulfilled.

George Pocaterra, the original owner of the Buffalo Head Ranch, planned to mine a deposit on Evans-Thomas Creek. The deposit was expected to yield at least 125,000 tons of recoverable coal. In 1910, Pocaterra leased 1370 hectares in the Evans-Thomas Creek area, but when he discovered the cost of mining and transporting the coal to Calgary, he abandoned the project. Now, the only remainders of the early days of coal exploration and development in the Elbow/Sheep Wildland are a few relics on the site of the old Burns Mine, which is still held as private land.

Bolstered by the incentive of steadily increasing numbers of tourists, the fledgling Rocky Mountains National Park was expanded in 1902 to cover 12 691 square kilometres, including the entire western portion of the Elbow/Sheep Wildland. In 1911, the park was drastically reduced in size, to 4662 square kilometres. The Elbow/Sheep lands were dropped from the park only to be again included by boundaries that encompassed the entire Kananaskis drainage in 1917. Then in 1930, these lands were omitted for the final time, reverting to the Bow River division of the Rocky Mountain National Forest, which had been established in 1911. Having been deleted from the national park, the Kananaskis drainage lands, along with those of the Spray River, were managed as a game reserve until the mid-1950s. A 1927 National Forest Service pamphlet boldly contains subtitles "No Forests - No Game", "No Forests - No Camping", and "No Forests - No Fishing" for the Bow River National Forest which "each year witnesses an increase in the number of restseekers that migrate to these solitudes." The pamphlet describes this 5530 square kilometre forest reserve as having 724 kilometres of primary trails and an even larger number of secondary and auxiliary trails that could be used by horse packtrains to reach "the more inaccessible corners of the forest." Those pack trails included a network in the Elbow/Sheep, with trails along today's Highway 40, the Sheep, Little Elbow and Elbow rivers, from the Sheep River through Rickert's Pass and down Mist Creek, and through Elbow Pass.

Into the 1930s there was only one "permanent" forest ranger and one assistant ranger hired during the fire season for the entire Bow River National Forest. Although called "permanent", these rangers were laid off during the winter months and given their choice of trap line areas. These men were combination game guardians, fish and wildlife managers, foresters and fire fighters.

During this early Forest Service period, each year the cowboys and guests at Buffalo Head Ranch would help stock the Highwood's tributaries with fish. It was, according to former owner R.M. Patterson,

. . . always good for a lively day. The dudes would go off with Sam, our district fishery warden, on the morning of the day the Fishery Department tank-truck came up the valley loaded with thousands . . . of trout fry for the stocking of Flat Creek [Trap Creek] and Sullivan Creek. The truck would go as far as it could; then the Buffalo Head packhorses would take over. The fry would be transferred into cans with ice containers and with wire gauze, sacking-covered lids to allow the passage of air, and the horses would stand quietly while these were loaded on them and secured. Things, however, always livened up a bit the moment the party moved off: the unaccustomed glugging of the water in the fish can never failed to alarm and excite the horses who would tear around in circles on the end of their lead ropes with a horseman hanging on to each one, pivoting on his horse and trying to quieten him. Sometimes a frantic packhorse would wrap his lead rope and himself round a tree; or else two lead ropes would tangle and two horses jam together with the full equivalent of a typhoon on the Pacific taking place inside the fish cans. This annual circus of Sam's was always a popular event in the calendar – and, strange to say, the mortality amongst the fry was never very great. After two or three miles of some foothill pack trail, the fish cans would be decanted into a likely looking pool. A few tiny bodies would float to the surface – but a brown cloud of swarming, active life would show for a moment in the clear water and then vanish, seemingly none the worse for their wild ride.

The eastern portion of the Elbow/Sheep still remains within the Forest Reserve, with the upper Kananaskis drainage and Highwood Pass segment once again a park - this time part of Kananaskis Provincial Park.

Wildlife

At one time buffalo roamed into the Elbow/ Sheep. Complete skeletons were once found on the side of Mist Mountain. In the late 1800s, encroaching civilization took its toll on wildlife in this region. Extensive fires, attitudes of the day which rated all predators as bad, the influx of settlers, and the demise of the buffalo which turned the attention of meat and sport hunters to other game, all combined to destroy many animals and their habitat.

The establishment of the Kananaskis Game Reserve and regrowth after the fires aided the recovery of ungulates, but all predators were actively destroyed. The encroachment of ranching and settlement brought demise to the Elbow/Sheep grizzly bear population by the 1950s. Today, these magnificent creatures which once inhabited lands from the mountains to the plains now maintain a foothold to the west in the heart of Kananaskis Provincial Park. If their habitat can be maintained, there is hope that individual bears will again establish in the wilderness lands of the Elbow/Sheep.

The Elbow/Sheep lands provide quality habitat for mountain and foothill animals such as bighorn sheep, mountain goat, elk, moose and mule deer. Relatively recently, feral horses and white-tail deer have also moved in from the east. The recent closure of the road running·through the headwaters of the Elbow and Sheep rivers will no doubt further enhance wildlife use of the available habitat.

Elk, shy by nature, thrive in large tracts of wilderness. Thus the lush, extensive grasslands in the Elbow/Sheep Wildland provide quality range for them. The area encompasses critical habitat for mountain goats and critical winter habitat for both the elk and bighorn sheep. Such important areas include those around The Wedge and Evans-Thomas Creek valley, Cliff Creek, Gibralter Mountain, Mist Ridge and Mist Mountain, Cougar Mountain, Threepoint Mountain, Mount Rose, Missing Link Mountain, Mount Head and Volcano Ridge. The Wedge/ Evans-Thomas area, which provides year-round habitat for bighorn sheep, elk and mountain goat, is considered one of the most important of the critical wildlife ranges in the Eastern Slopes. A wildlife sanctuary has been in place since 1973 along the Sheep River in the area of Missing Link Mountain and Mount Hoffman to protect wintering populations of bighorn sheep.

Mountain goats live in the seclusion of the rocky peaks of the Fisher Range. Moose are well distributed through the area and are often seen at lower elevations, lumbering through meadows or feeding on woody shrubs and water plants. Occasionally, in summer, insects and heat drive them up into the shrubby alpine areas.

Mule deer browse in the willow flats found along the foothill valleys of the Highwood, Sheep and Elbow rivers and Trap Creek. They too seek the relief of higher elevations in the summer. White-tail deer tend to inhabit the eastern fringes of the Elbow/Sheep.

The proposed Elbow/Sheep Wildland Recreation Area also provides sufficient territory for large predators like the black bear, wolf, coyote, lynx, bobcat and cougar. The home range of female cougars, for example, averages 250 square kilometres, while range for the male averages 450 square kilometres. The lynx, a long-legged member of the cat family, depends on the snowshoe hare for food and inhabits the thick timber and deadfall of the mature forests. The lynx is sometimes confused with the bobcat, which is smaller and prefers the more open grassland habitat.

Small carnivores found in the area include marten, mink, fishers, skunks, weasels and wolverines. The mink hunts at night and is seldom seen. With luck the tree-dwelling marten can sometimes be seen darting along tree branches hunting squirrels. Wolverines are not commonly seen but do populate these wilderness lands. Re-introduced in Kananaskis Country, river otters and fishers now inhabit their former range in the Elbow/Sheep.

The proposed Wildland Recreation Area is home to many birds, with over 240 species having been recorded. These include the native upland game birds: blue grouse, spruce grouse and white-tailed ptarmigan. The blue grouse winters in the evergreen forests near timberline, feeding primarily on needles and buds. In the spring, this grouse returns to lightly wooded areas, where the male struts, defining his territory and vying for female attention.

Golden eagles and winter wrens which nest in the area are indicators of the remnant mature subalpine forests that can be found in the Elbow/Sheep. The area also has a mixing of eastern and western birds. For example, the Steller's jay is found here at its eastern limit, and the boblink also occurs here at the western limit of its range.

Fishery

Cutthroat trout, bull trout, rainbow trout, eastern brook trout and Rocky Mountain Whitefish are all found within the waters of the Elbow/Sheep area. However, fishing demand is too great for the size of the natural population, so all the high mountain lakes are stocked with cutthroat, and many lakes and streams are also stocked with rainbow trout. The most widely known of the trout family, rainbow trout are native to the Athabasca River system of northern Alberta and have done well when stocked in lakes and streams further south. An assortment of beaver ponds and man-made ponds along the roads bordering the Elbow/Sheep are stocked as well.

At the present time, most streams in the wilderness area are classified as poor in terms of trout productivity. This is attributable to water level fluctuations, insufficient pools, sparse bottom fauna, constant scouring and shifting of the river channels, absence of streamside vegetation and a lack of variation in streambed composition. Also, some stream damage has occurred from road and seismic line incursions. Nevertheless, the potential fishery is rated as excellent to outstanding, subject to instituting and carrying out steam improvement and rehabilitation projects. Experimental work and research studies regarding native and introduced fish species have been conducted at Gorge Creek for many years.

A number of creeks such as Ware, Threepoint and Trap creeks are spawning areas for rainbow and brook trout. Rocky Mountain whitefish are among the most numerous of the game fish in the area, preferring larger creeks and rivers like Prairie and Canyon creeks and the Highwood River.

Vegetation

The Elbow/Sheep encompasses parkland, foothills and mountain vegetation. Vegetation patterns have been overshadowed by a violent fire history. Generally, changes in vegetation correspond to changes in elevation, with parkland and coniferous forests at lower elevation and sweeping alpine tundra at high elevations.

For the most part, the Elbow/Sheep is situated in the front ranges and foothills of the Rockies, which are in a rain shadow, characterized by lower precipitation than the higher main ranges to the west.

In the eastern foothills, fingers of fescue grassland extend west into a few valley bottoms.

Sweet-smelling willow, aspen and balsam poplar freshen creek valleys and are interspersed with willow, grass and sedge meadows.

Major fires occurred throughout the late 1800s and early 1900s. The last major fire began in 1936 in the Elk Valley in British Columbia and swept east through Weary Creek Gap on the Continental Divide, and went on to engulf the Kananaskis, Highwood, Elbow and Sheep valleys. These fires burned much of the original spruce/alpine fir forest of the high elevation foothills and lower mountain slopes, leaving only mature stands with their feather moss understory tucked away in the upper reaches of valleys. Fire successional lodgepole pine forests are thus common, as are vast tracts of dry windswept slopes dotted with the charred stumps of the original spruce/fir forests. Reed grass, hairy wild rye, fireweed, calypso orchids and bunchberry brighten the floor of the pine forests. Young stands of spruce and alpine fir mixed with lodgepole pine are also frequent. The plant understory of these forests varies greatly depending on the age of the particular forest. Flowers such as twin-flower, evergreen violet, star-flowered Solomon's seal, heart-leaved arnica, buttercup and several native orchids tend to be more predominant in the younger of these forests.

Perhaps the most unusual and interesting vegetation of the Elbow/Sheep is the partially forested parkland occurring on the innermost foothills and lower mountains. It provides excellent elk and deer habitat and is extensively used for cattle grazing. Sunny, south-facing slopes and ridge crests are carpeted with grasses, such as hairy wild rye, northern awnless brome, fescue, bluegrass and kobresia. These are the lands which provide critical winter range for bighorn sheep and elk.

At timberline, the forest breaks up into islands of dwarfed Engelmann spruce and alpine fir, interspersed with lush meadows. These meadows are a colourful delight throughout their short growing season, beginning in spring with yellow carpets of glacier lilies, bold white globe-flowers and western anemonies. Communities of white mountain avens and dwarf willow are spectacular in early spring as a multitude of alpine flowers begin the growing season. The list of common flowers includes white mountain avens, alpine forget-me-not, Lyall's ironplant, golden fleabane, rock-jasmine, alpine cinquefoil, purple saxifrage, moss campion and alpine arnica. Next to bloom are the heather communities dominated by purple, white and yellow mountain heathers. Also at timberline grow the graceful white-bark pine and in more sheltered areas the alpine larch. On exposed ridge crests grow wind-pruned Douglas fir and picturesque limber pine as well as colourful alpine flowers.

Early autumn in the Elbow/Sheep is marked by the brilliant colors of the landscape. In mountain meadows, the alpine bearberry turns vivid crimson. On alpine slopes, communities of sedge, the favourite food of the bighorn sheep and mountain goat, turn a rich yellow hue. Later on, the alpine larch turns a brilliant gold and orange before shedding its feathery needles.

There are presently two small candidate Ecological Reserves within the Elbow/Sheep Wildland. The proposed 2072 hectare Upper Evans-Thomas is representative of the Rocky Mountain montane vegetation zone, and the 648 hectare Elbow/Sheep Divide is representative of alpine and subalpine vegetation.

Recreation

Located within an hour's drive of the major metropolitan centre of Calgary, the wilderness lands of the Elbow/Sheep are invaluable and greatly enhance the desirability of living in the Calgary area. The Elbow/Sheep's extremely scenic, rugged mountain wilderness, abundant wildlife, clean waters, ample size and network of trails make it ideally suited to all forms of wilderness recreation. It has been popular for recreation since the first pack trails, later followed by roads, went into the area in the early 1900s.

Many visitors are lured to the Elbow/Sheep by high quality opportunities for non-motorized recreation, which range from trail riding, backpacking or hiking to fishing, hunting and commercially outfitted trips. The Elbow/Sheep presents the visitor with a broad spectrum of mountain and foothills wilderness landscapes. Although close to Calgary, the area still provides quiet solitude and is of sufficient size for wilderness trips of more than four days. Spring comes earlier to the Elbow/Sheep than to Banff National Park in the main mountain ranges further west, allowing a longer season for trips by foot or horse.

The Elbow/Sheep now falls within Kananaskis Country, a multi-million-dollar recreation development project of the Alberta government. The Spray River drainage and the western portion of the Kananaskis drainage, including Kananaskis Provincial Park, have been developed to provide major facilities for outdoor and urban type recreation pursuits. Facilities such as restaurants, a fully serviced recreation vehicle

campground complete with cable T.V. hook-ups, two alpine ski resorts, a golf course, service stations, numerous day-use sites, a number of campgrounds, a lodge for the handicapped and two youth hostels can be found in the lands surrounding the Elbow/Sheep wilderness. Given protection, the Elbow/Sheep as a wilderness beginning on the east side of the Kananaskis River will complete the spectrum of opportunities Kananaskis Country could offer visitors. As part of Kananaskis Country, the Elbow/Sheep should be carefully managed to protect its wilderness value.

Hiking and Horseback Riding

Through the decades, a network of foot and horse trails have developed within the Elbow/Sheep, beginning with the ancient Indian trails, and followed by those of the early forest service, range riders and outfitters. With topographic maps in hand, numerous interesting trips of one overnight or longer can be planned, beginning from any side of the Elbow/Sheep boundary.

With the development of Kananaskis Country, motorized use within the Elbow/Sheep was closed, with the exception of snowmobile use around Sibbald Flats. However, unfortunately, the gravel-base road running through the headwaters of the Elbow and Sheep rivers has yet to be reclaimed. With the Kananaskis Country recreation project, equestrian and foot trails were formally developed in the eastern or Gorge Creek area of the Elbow/Sheep, most of which follow old seismic lines or truck trails. Some trail development or "upgrading" also took place along the Little

Elbow, Elbow and Sheep rivers and Mist Creek valley, with four backcountry campgrounds being constructed in these areas. However, for the most part, the Elbow/Sheep remains very much a wilderness with few man-made intrusions.

There are 15 developed vehicle access campgrounds within 10 kilometres of the Elbow/Sheep's boundaries, providing over 1,200 sites. Many of these campsites are excellent staging areas for trips into the Wildland. Two youth hostels and a camp and lodge for the handicapped are also in the vicinity of the Elbow/Sheep.

Road access, much of it by means of high-standard highways, is provided to all sides of the Elbow/Sheep. Highway 40 from the Kananaskis Park gate south to the Highwood Junction is closed each winter season from December 1 to June 15th in order to protect critical wildlife winter habitat. The Elbow River road upstream of Elbow Falls, the Sheep River road upstream of Coal Creek and the Ford Creek road are closed from December 1st to May 15th.

Climbing

A number of peaks in the Elbow/Sheep Wildland provide challenges to novice, intermediate and experienced mountaineers. Local ranchers were the first to climb many of the peaks in the Highwood Range, with first ascents of those peaks over 3000 metres recorded in 1946. Among the peaks of interest to climbers in the Storm Creek/Pocaterra Creek area are Mount Rae (3218 metres), Mount Arethusa (2912 metres), Storm Mountain (3091 metres), or Mist Mountain (3140 metres). Other climbing peaks include those in the Opal Range, such as Tombstone

Mountain (3035 metres), Elpoca Mountain (3029 metres), Mount Jerram (2996 metres), Mount Burney (2934 metres), Mount Packenham (3000 metres) and Mount Evans-Thomas (3097 metres). East of the Opal Range are Mount Glasgow (2935 metres), Mount Cornwall (2970 metres) and Banded Peak (2934 metres). Climbing possibilities in the Fisher Range include Fisher Peak (3053 metres), Mount Howard (2777 metres) and Mount McDougall (2726 metres). Mount Head (2782 metres) in the Highwood Range is also of potential interest to climbers.

Fishing and Hunting

The Elbow/Sheep provides a variety of stream and high mountain lake fishing. Due to low productivity of the region's waters, most are stocked.

The Palliser Expedition more than 100 years ago made reference to the fine fishing in the Highwood River, which touches on the southern flank of the Elbow/Sheep Wildland. The original excellent fishing conditions in the Kananaskis Lakes and Kananaskis River bordering the wilderness area on the west have all but been destroyed by hydro-electric power installations. This once-productive watershed at one time contributed significantly to the food supply of the Stoney Indians. Lakes such as Burns, Rae, Elbow and Lower Tombstone, as well as Upper Ford Creek, are stocked with cutthroat trout.

Rainbow trout are stocked in Forget-Me-Not and Powderface ponds as well as in Ford Creek. Both rainbow and eastern brook trout are stocked in beaver ponds of the Highwood and Elbow

rivers as well as Ford, Wasootch, Storm, Picklejar and Cat creeks.

A member of the char family, eastern brook trout has also been stocked in the north and south forks of Prairie Creek and in upper Stoney Creek as well as Elbow Lake. Bull trout and Rocky Mountain whitefish may also be fished in the Highwood River and Prairie and Canyon creeks.

In terms of a recreational type of wilderness, fishing is an activity which should be encouraged. It is an excellent use of a renewable resource, is non-polluting, non-facility oriented and is sufficiently inexpensive to be within the budget of most Albertans. The thrill of a strike on the line or the pleasure of fresh trout cooked over an open fire can provide an added dimension to an exhilarating day of wilderness travel.

Closure of motorized use within the Elbow/Sheep has now provided top quality wilderness hunting opportunities. This has resulted in a recent upsurge in the popularity of hunting in the Elbow/Sheep area, especially for big game. A number of guides and outfitters provide full service into these wilderness lands.

Land Use Concerns and Recommendations

The proposed Elbow/Sheep Wildland Recreation Area is the only large, relatively undisturbed natural area within Kananaskis Country. With the exception of a zone for facility development at the Wedge Pond/Evans-Thomas area and the eastern boundary area, the majority of the Elbow/Sheep is proposed as Prime Protection Zone lands by Alberta government planning. The eastern boundary area is planned as a mixture of Multiple Use zone permitting the full spectrum of industrial activities, and General Recreation zone, which permits recreation facility development. The Critical Wildlife zoning of lands at the Wedge/Evans-Thomas, Volcano Creek, and the Sheep River Sanctuary, and of lands surrounding Mount Head may also prove to be cause for concern. Industrial activities could be permitted where they do not interfere with wildlife management objectives. The focus should be on full protection of the wilderness and wildlife attributes of these lands.

Coal, Oil and Gas, Minerals

Besides the Burns Mine established for a short time in the early 1900s, most activity has consisted of geological mapping and seismic work. There are no plans to permit the development of the relatively limited coal reserves within the Elbow/Sheep. However, the 9.7 square kilometres of the Burns Mine site is still private land.

The only exploratory drilling for petroleum and natural gas in the area was conducted in 1959 near Banded Peak but was abandoned after drilling 3144 metres without a commercial strike. Three sour gas fields (West Jumping Pound, Moose Mountain and Quirk Creek) are near the eastern boundary of the area, and thus there is some potential for further exploration and development into the proposed Wildland Recreation Area. However, all but the eastern

boundary area of the Elbow/Sheep lies west of the McConnell Thrust Fault, denoting no known potential for oil and gas. Present government policy would permit oil and gas development from existing fields to extend into the Prime Protection lands.

There are no quariable or metallic minerals of commercial interest within the area.

Timber

Timber resources are not extensive within the Elbow/Sheep Wildland. Trees are slow growing because of the high elevations and the associated poor growing climate. Past fires have left few areas with mature timber of commercial size.

The limited amount of land zoned as Multiple Use, General Recreation and Critical Wildlife within the Elbow/Sheep is considered to be part of the land base permanently available for commercial logging. Thus there presently is the potential that mature stands within these areas would be harvested, and the more extensive young timber could be harvested in the future.

The Rock, Volcano, Gorge and Blue Rock creek areas, however, have been withdrawn from the permanent timber land base due to the steep ridges and incised valleys which prohibit normal logging access.

Grazing

Brush and aspen encroachment onto grasslands precipitated by the control of fires since 1936 has resulted in a considerable reduction in grassland. A program of controlled burning

should be considered as an aid to regaining grassland, especially critical winter range for elk and bighorn sheep.

There are a number of cattle-grazing allotments located primarily in the eastern boundary area of the Elbow/Sheep. Climatic and topographic features limit the availability of grass for domestic use within the vast majority of the Elbow/Sheep.

The Sheep Creek winds its way through a steep-banked valley.

Upper Kananaskis
Guidance from History

In 1914, M.C. Hendry compiled a technical report for the federal Department of the Interior from his "Bow River Power and Storage Investigations". While assigned to report on potential dam sites for the Kananaskis Lakes, he wrote:

The upper lake is worthy of special mention from a scenic point of view – it is studded with islands and has snow-capped mountains to form a backdrop, the addition of well-timbered shores and islands forms a picture which rivals in beauty any of the better-known lakes which are to be found in the Rockies . . . The fishing in these two lakes is excellent . . . in considering any scheme of storage on this lake (the upper lake), the beauty of the lake in its natural state and the extreme probability of its becoming a summer resort in the near future should not be lost sight of.

With the large and increasing numbers of people who seek unmarred mountain landscapes, Albertans could use those once-breathtaking lakes of the Kananaskis now. But despite the foresight of Mr. Hendry some 70 years ago, the Kananaskis Lakes have been replaced by storage reservoirs.

Logging operations begun in 1883, dams first built on the Kananaskis Lakes in 1932, coal exploration and mines, gypsum exploration, a downhill ski development and construction of a major highway had by 1973 stripped all the wilderness from the Kananaskis Valley, save for a 130 square kilometre remnant encompassing the headwaters which now feed the Upper Kananaskis Lake reservoir.

Resource development has also taken with it our chance to map the ancient history of the Kananaskis. Salvage excavations in front of the advancing construction of Highway 40 unearthed some 5,000 artifacts dating back to around 5500 B.C.

As small as this pocket of wilderness may be, its glaciers, 17 peaks reaching over 3050 metres and four alpine lakes are still as spectacular as when the Kootenay Indians used the North and South Kananaskis passes. Until the 1850s these passes were the Kootenay's most direct route between their settlements at Canal Flats and the

Upper Kananaskis Lake, photographed in 1911 by George Pocaterra. This breathtaking vista was all but eliminated by the construction of storage reservoirs in the 1930s.

campsites were built into the Upper Kananaskis to encourage and accommodate the large number of visitors that could now be brought to the area by high standard highways and the recreation facility developments of Kananaskis Country.

While driving down the wide highway of the Smith-Dorrien Valley or sipping on a cool drink at the Boulton Creek Restaurant, it may be hard to visualize that you are within Alberta's "Wildland Park". However, brochures promise,

> These areas will not be developed extensively, but will be left as wild and as natural as possible . . . You'll be largely on your own in wildland class parks - far from the comforts of home, except for those you carry with you!

As a goal to attain, the statements forecast a brighter future for the Highwood Pass critical elk winter range, the Smith-Dorrien Valley grizzly habitat, the Elk Passes and British Columbia's Elk Lakes Provincial Park (which were on the drawing board for a major interprovincial highway), and the Upper Kananaskis itself.

Our wilderness and wildland resources require careful and wise management under the guidance of legislated protection. The more than half a billion dollars of public funds that have been spent on the Kananaskis Country Recreation Development project have not replaced the Kananaskis Lakes which once rivalled the wild beauty of any of the better known Rocky Mountain lakes. Heeding the lessons of our past, we must act today to protect our remaining Eastern Slopes wilderness lands.

Eastern Slope hunting areas which included their favourite elk hunting grounds at the Kananaskis Lakes.

In 1973, the Alberta Wilderness Association proposed protection for this little wilderness jewel as the Upper Kananaskis Wildland Recreation Area.

In 1977, it was included as part of the present Kananaskis Provincial Park, the core of the Kananaskis Country recreation area.

Descriptions of the park including the Upper Kananaskis can now be found in the pamphlets, maps and books put out on Kananaskis Country.

Provincial Park status brought the needed legislated protection from resource industry development to the Upper Kananaskis. But for wilderness enthusiasts, this came with a price: that of recreation development. High standard trails, a warden's cabin and backcountry

Upper Oldman
A Family's Wilderness

The sharp crack of splitting wood in the crisp mountain dawn rang the morning alarm. Curiosity about the day ahead was enough incentive to roll out of my cosy down bag and fling the tent flap open to have a look. Yawns soon gave way to the irresistable smell of sizzling bacon and the magic aroma of fresh coffee mingling with the high country air. The day's plans were formulated and scrutinized over the morning coffee. While the sun warmed the dew off the greenery, each of us went off to attend to the day's preparations.

With the relatives visiting from out-of-province and each of us looking for a week's holiday with our own ideal mixture of wild mountain scenery, adventure and relaxation in

mind, the Upper Oldman was the logical place to be for the family camping trip. Heading "back to the wilds" started with a turn west off the Forestry Trunk Road and followed a rutted gravel road up along the northwest branch of the Oldman River. No paved road, no planned campground stalls or conventional motor home "hook-ups" here. Visitors to the Upper Oldman wouldn't want it any other way. Each of us chose our favourite random camping spot, tucked somewhere along the 28 kilometre road. On route, we passed several makeshift signs set up so friends and family could find the right campsite. On this trip, one piece of cardboard read "Heaven Sent Rest Area - fishing, camping, hiking, horseshoes and relaxation." Amen to that!

Dad and my brother-in-law re-appeared with their favourite battered old fishing hats on their heads and fly rods in their hands. "Just off to check how the Dollies and cutthroats are doing." Referring to his favourite set of fast-flowing trout streams since boyhood, Dad's words had a ring of urgency these days. These native beauties of clear flowing mountain brooks are in jeopardy elsewhere. Logging and mining practices, and cattle-damaged stream banks elsewhere in Alberta have left few healthy populations of cutthroat and bull trout. My Dad knew that the extended road access here had brought too many people for the good of the fishing and once-renowned big game hunting.

Mom and my sister decided they'd hang around camp, relax in the sunshine, catch up

on some reading and watch the river flow by.
Maybe they'd hike up to the windblown limber
pine on Pasque Ridge and take in some of the
superb scenes of the Upper Oldman valley later
in the afternoon. Lawnchairs were pulled out to
just the right spot under the watchful eye of
Beehive Mountain, and the bird guide was
flopped down within easy reach.

As for my young nephews and I, we had plans
that fit into a larger scheme. For us it'd be a long
day hike, a trial run for an overnight backpack
trip planned for later in the week. Our
destination would be a high ridge offering an
expansive view into the Hidden Creek
headwaters – sights sure to tantalize my nephews'
appetites for their first backpacking trip.

While wading across the cold waters of the
Oldman River, the frigid waters from the mouth
of Cache Creek numbed the feet and triggered
thoughts of high alpine snow patches shimmering
white in the brilliant sunshine. But this wasn't
any "matter of course" river crossing. On the
other side lay a *de facto* wilderness, the scenic
backdrop for those camped along the Oldman
River. The area we were crossing into is the last
intact wilderness land along the southern main
range of the Canadian Rockies, with the
exception of the crowded confines protected
inside Waterton Lakes National Park to the
south. The Wildland's significance was felt as
much as the cold water swirling around our legs.

Steps along the age-old trail following Cache
Creek were accompanied by young imaginations
picturing the ancient hunters who had travelled
the three passes of the Upper Oldman area.
Stones in the meadow along the trail conjured
thoughts of the teepee rings left by their spring

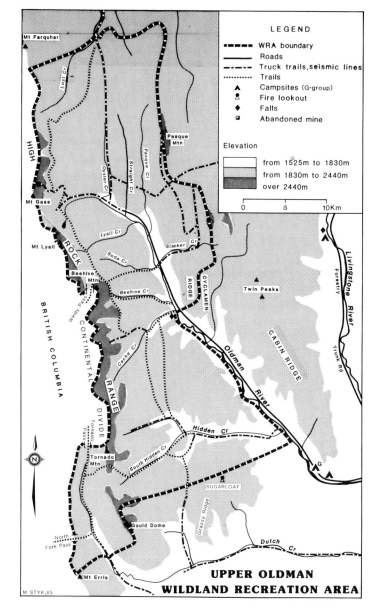

LEGEND

▪▪▪▪ WRA boundary
────── Roads
─·─·─ Truck trails, seismic lines
······· Trails
▲ Campsites (G-group)
🛈 Fire lookout
◆ Falls
▣ Abandoned mine

Elevation

from 1525m to 1830m
from 1830m to 2440m
over 2440m

0   5   10Km

M STYK, 85

**UPPER OLDMAN
WILDLAND RECREATION AREA**

and fall hunting camps, and of the meat caches for which the creek was named.

Muscles tired from the climb were quickly forgotten when we clambered to the top of the ridge. Two boys scampered like young mountain sheep along the ridge walk, rushing to each new blossom that caught their eye, then spinning around to point at the peaks towering above them. Spread below us lay undulating hills clothed in the deep green silver-tipped velvet of an old growth subalpine forest, a surprising and welcome panorama in the southern Rockies where all other sizable tracks of Forest Reserve land have been logged. It was almost as if we had discovered what we thought had been lost years ago, as if unknowingly we'd given ourselves one more chance to save a part of our heritage.

The trees in the Hidden Creek sub-basin spread out before us were about 275 years old when in 1858, Captain Blakiston of the Palliser Expedition looked west from the foothills through the Livingstone Gap to name the dome-shaped peak above us "Gould's Dome". Hidden amongst those trees are the mineral licks and well worn trails of one of Alberta's largest elk herds.

There's scarcely been a trip that I've made into this spot without seeing a rainbow. In 1915, while surveying the provincial boundary in this area, the Interprovincial Boundary Commission concluded that Gould's Dome's new name of Tornado Mountain was "certainly appropriate, for it is a storm centre." On the occasion of two ascents, their party narrowly escaped death at the hands of its storied disposition. Then on one occasion, "while on a peak across the valley, a wonderfully vivid double rainbow encircled Tornado Mountain . . . ."

Now, 70 years later, their description of the area still holds true. "The south approach to Tornado Pass is particularly attractive; meadow-like flower-clad glades, in which flow little crystal streams, interspersed with open belts of graceful spruce and larch trees which charm the eye. The pass summit is most picturesque and grandly impressive in its surroundings. The precipice of Tornado Mountain rises 2,500 feet; gigantic rock buttresses stand out, separated by huge cavernous chimneys and the general effect is awe inspiring."

Approaching camp at the end of the day, we spotted everyone high on the river cutbank watching what we thought was us. Approaching the river crossing, we could see that everyone was really watching a cow and calf moose crossing through our swimming hole in the bend of the river.

Supper was waiting for us as the sun set. In the warmth of the evening campfire, talk of the day's adventures ebbed and flowed with the crackling of the fire. Eyes were held captive by dancing embers. Finishing off a handful of popcorn, one of the boys piped up, "I sure like this park, Grandpa!" Somehow, we didn't have the heart to tell him park status was still to be won.

In the 1930s, one of Alberta's first outfitters, Bert Riggall, was asked by a client to find the most beautiful spot in the Canadian Rockies for a family packing trip. Riggall chose the headwaters of the Oldman River. His choice was not a casual one. Bert Riggall was also the person who gave Kootenay Brown photos of the Waterton Lakes area to aid in Brown's bid to have Waterton protected as a national park.

The Continental Divide, the highest ranges of the Rocky Mountains which divide waters flowing to the Pacific from those flowing to the Atlantic, is the backbone of the proposed Upper Oldman Wildland Recreation Area. Uniquely shaped peaks such as Beehive Mountain and the Gauntlet, as well as the highest peak in the southern Rockies, Tornado Mountain, are part of the "High Rock" chain of Continental Divide peaks which form the western boundary of Alberta and the proposed Wildland Recreation Area. This wilderness encompasses the headwaters of a major river which bears a derivation of the Indian name Napi-och-a-tay-cots or "Where the Old Man plays" - "God's Paradise". It is truly an area of outstanding beauty.

In recent times the Upper Oldman has taken on a special provincial significance as it is the only substantial, relatively undisturbed tract of land left in Alberta's south Rocky Mountains outside of the federal Waterton Lakes National Park. Interestingly, the major pine and spruce insect infestations which swept through the region in the 1970s and early 1980s have by-passed the old growth forests of the Upper Oldman.

The visitor to this 300 square kilometre wilderness will find open grassy meadows and cool, dark, subalpine forests intersected by clear, fast-flowing trout streams. In the high elevation forests have been found what may be Alberta's largest Engelmann spruce and whitebark pine trees. The inquisitive visitor will also find clues to a rich and diverse history of Alberta's Eastern Slopes.

In these ancient forests, pine siskins and grosbeaks call, while above the treeline a profusion of delicate flowering alpine plants unfold in mid-summer against a backdrop of wind-swept scree slopes and rugged peaks. Through these landscapes roam bighorn sheep, mountain goats, grizzly bear and one of Alberta's largest elk herds.

A 2½ hour drive southwest from Calgary or an hour north from Highway 3, the Upper Oldman reflects the urgency with which wilderness landscapes must be protected in Alberta. Its growing popularity and its provincial significance have led the Alberta Wilderness Association to seek legislative protection of its important headwaters from impending large-scale logging operations, potential coal development, mineral exploration and present off-highway vehicle use.

Geology

Light grey limestones and dolomites up to some 395 million years old were dramatically thrust upward and eastward, faulted and folded to form the rugged High Rock Range of the western portion of the Upper Oldman. On the east lie much younger rock strata of sandstones and dark grey marine shales folding into gently dipping anticlines and synclines. Creek valleys in the area cut through these Upper Cretaceous sandstones and shales. Northwest/southeast-trending ridges in the southeast portion of the

Upper Oldman are underlain with relatively resistant outcrops of older Mesozoic strata of the Lower Cretaceous and Jurasic ages. This area, encompassing Pasque Mountain and Cabin Ridge just across the Oldman River from the proposed Wildland Recreation Area, includes the coal-bearing Kootenay formation. Most of the area was probably disturbed by the three glacial advances which moved down from the alpine slopes of the mountains into lower elevations, sculpting mountainside cirques and broadening the stream-cut Oldman River valley into a U-shape. Studies of vegetation in the Beehive Mountain segment reveal that some small areas may not have been glaciated during the last ice age, thus acting as refugium for plants until the neighboring ice retreated.

Human History

The marks left through time by man on the wilderness landscapes of the Upper Oldman today provide a living history of Alberta's Rocky Mountain region. Due to this area's relatively undisturbed nature, it is still possible to read from the land each chapter of that history. To camp in the meadows along the upper reaches of the Oldman River is to forge a link to nearly 9,000 years of human history. Archaeologists had only a fleeting opportunity to examine the pristine areas before seismic lines and the road along the Oldman River were constructed. They found evidence that ancient tribes of native people seasonally occupied the valleys of the Upper Oldman. Evidence of their spring and fall

hunting camps were found at the Oldman River tributary junctions of Oyster, Hayden, Honeymoon, Cache and Slacker creeks as well as on the upper section of Dutch Creek. Tornado Pass and Windy Pass on the Continental Divide, along with the Oyster Creek Pass between the Highwood and Oldman River watershed, are well-worn ancient trails.

In 1884, George Dawson, a pioneering Dominion government land surveyor, noticed rock cairns used as markers by Kootenay Indians crossing the Highwood/Oldman watershed divide from Lost Creek to Oyster Creek. The Interprovincial Boundary Commission of 1915 reported the wide, well worn pack trail up Dutch Creek from North Fork Pass to Tornado Pass in a state of abandonment and disrepair. Although the very long trail blazes cut into the trees have since disappeared, the trappers, guides, range riders and forest rangers who followed repaired and incorporated these ancient trails into their own trail systems. These trails provide today's traveller with a route to our natural and cultural past.

Cache Creek was named for the meat caches kept there by the native peoples. The Stoneys hunted and camped throughout the Upper Oldman until early in this century, maintaining a proprietary interest in the area. The Upper Oldman is thus steeped in the Stoney's heritage.

With the Dominion government's establishment of the Crowsnest National Forest in 1911, forest rangers were assigned all the fire fighting as well as fish and wildlife, forest and range management duties in the area. Among the list of "more important" duties was the construction and maintenance of trails. The Indian trails in the Upper Oldman were cleared of deadfall and new trails were opened. A cabin was constructed near the junction of Cache Creek and the Oldman River. Forest Service maps from the 1930s have the locations of these trails along with the common local names still in use, such as "Profanity Creek" (Pasque Creek) and Panorama Mountain (Pasque Mountain).

Prospectors combed this wilderness for the gold of the Lost Lemon Mine. Determined fortune-seekers followed the "Northwest Branch" or Oldman River to its end and scaled nearby mountains in search of mineral wealth. They found galena, a mixture of lead, silver and zinc. Undeterred by the remoteness of the area, they developed Miracle Mine and widened the trail along the Oldman River into a cart trail. The metal ore was packed out of the area in horse-drawn wagons until the early 1920s when the galena in the chimney formation ran out. The mine's crumbling shafts and a derelict ore car which toppled to the valley below remain at the Miracle Mine site on the face of Mount Gass.

In 1916, a group of First World War draft evaders built a cabin near the creek subsequently named Slacker Creek. The slackers' cabin was later abandoned but outfitter Bert Riggall by 1920 had begun using it as a base for his summer and fall outfitting in the Upper Oldman wilderness.

One of his typical fall outfitting trips in the 1920s would begin from the Riggall ranch on Cottonwood Creek near Twin Butte and set off with team and wagon and a string of around 25 horses. The hunting party, usually from the Canadian east or northeastern United States, would be met at the railway in Lundbreck. The second night would be spent camped at the

Livingstone Gap, and the base camp on Slacker Creek would be reached by the third evening. The major focus of most trips would be the spectacular wilderness scenery, trophy bighorn sheep hunting, trout fishing and some grizzly bear hunting. There were no major elk herds in the area until the 1940s.

During the Great Depression, a number of squatters and trappers attempted to eke out a meagre subsistance by hunting, fishing and trapping in the Upper Oldman region. Jack Morden, a successful old-time trapper, established a network of survival cabins throughout the Upper Oldman. Sifting through the remnants of one of Jack Morden's cabins on Hidden Creek, one can see the old trough roof design composed of hollowed logs laid to overlap like tiles.

During hard times, a make-work project for unemployed Crowsnest Pass coal miners was established on Hidden Creek. These "coal cabins" and others in the area were either lost to decay or were destroyed by the Forest Service out of concern that they presented a fire hazard or could be used as residences in an area where settlement is prohibited.

In the early 1900s, grazing allotments in the Upper Oldman were let out to ranchers, who then established a base camp cabin and corrals on Dutch Creek, with trails connecting into Hidden Creek and on through to the remainder of the Upper Oldman.

Exploration in the Wildland Recreation Area for mineral and forestry resources has varied over the years with market conditions. The cattle industry has operated continually throughout the century and has formed an economic base for neighbouring communities.

Wildlife and Vegetation

The only substantial tract of relatively undisturbed provincial land left in Alberta's southern Rocky Mountains, the wilderness lands of the Upper Oldman are noted for the summer habitat they provide for one of Alberta's largest elk herds, and for their old growth subalpine forests. This area's undisturbed forests in turn provide habitat for birds dependent on old growth forests and for a large variety of fur bearers. These lands also give rise to one of Alberta's top class trout fisheries, that of the Oldman River and its upper tributaries.

The majority of the Upper Oldman watershed is classed as subalpine and alpine, with 30 percent of the area above 1980 metres in elevation. These lands contain portions of three ecological regions, the alpine, subalpine and montane, with a number of vegetation types that can generally be grouped into alpine tundra, grassland, marsh, meadow, scrub and forest. The montane is very restricted, occurring only on the warmest, driest sites which are often on steep south-facing lower slopes. The alpine vegetation is diverse and contains species which are indicative of areas that were left unglaciated. At least eight species found in the Upper Oldman are rare in Alberta. The area may also be the northern range boundary for plant species which do not occur elsewhere in Alberta, except the southwest region.

Major fires ripped through the area in 1910 and 1936, accounting for the forest patterns seen today. Spreading through the lower valleys of the Oldman River and its tributaries and up over the Highwood/Oldman watershed divide, the upper watersheds were left untouched and are draped with old growth subalpine forests containing trees over 400 years old. At lower elevation, burned-over areas now have forests dominated by mature lodgepole pine. Above the 1980 metre elevation on the Highwood/Oldman watershed divide, the very sparce regrowth comprised of short trees gives the casual observer a clue as to how long it takes high elevation forests to grow.

In the valleys of the proposed Wildland Recreation Area, mule deer and moose move among the lodgepole pine, willow and sedge. A species of bluegrass, rare in Alberta, occurs in the subalpine grasslands of the lower valleys and southwest-facing slopes, while the uncommon squirreltail can be found in the scrub areas. Lincoln's sparrows, northern water thrushes, Swainson's thrushes and winter wrens seek the shade and food provided in these valleys. The proximity of streamside willow and dwarf birch thickets to coniferous forests makes prime breeding locations for song birds, including representatives of the warbler and thrush families. This vegetation type along the Oldman River valley also provides winter range for moose.

On slopes above 1950 metres exists a mixed coniferous forest of lodgepole pine, Engelmann spruce, alpine fir, alpine larch and white-bark pine with no one species dominant – an unusual if not unique forest. Very large Engelmann spruce up to 38 metres high and over a metre in diameter and a stand of equally large white-bark pine mixed with lodgepole pine occur in the Hidden Creek basin. These monarchs may well be the largest of their species living within Alberta. In the headwaters of Hidden Creek,

deep winter snows and the old growth forest give rise to very moist areas with giant lady ferns and streams that run all summer long among moss covered rocks. On north-facing slopes, under these old growth forest canopies grow white-flowered rhododendron, false huckleberry and low bilberry. A rare species of rattlesnake plantain is also found within these subalpine forests.

During the summer, tiny ruby-crowned and golden-crowned kinglets inhabit these forests. Red-breasted nuthatches can sometimes be seen creeping mouse-like down a tree. While Townsend's solitaires seize mayflies, the raucous calls of sociable grey jays and Clarke's nutcrackers reverberate among the peaks. The rufous hummingbird or his cousin the calliope hummingbird often flit through previously burned areas where fireweed abounds. The calliope is more commonly found west of the mountains in British Columbia.

Moist areas within these old growth forests are the habitat for three plants which rarely occur in Alberta, being confined to the extreme southwest region of the province: yellow angelica, sweet cicely and a species of chickweed. Moist meadows along at least one of the lakeshores are home to a rare species of willow herb.

Dwarf Engelmann spruce and alpine fir extend into the wind-ravaged alpine zone, yielding at higher elevations to wet meadows and snowbelt herbmats of sedges, glacier lilies and dwarf bilberry. Drier areas are dotted with white mountain avens, kobresia and mountain heathers. This landscape belongs to the golden eagle which might be seen swooping down upon a Columbian or golden mantled ground squirrel.

Above the tree line in the true alpine tundra, colourful mountain wildflowers like Indian paintbrush, fleabane, ragwort, gentian and columbine carpet the meadows during the brief mid-summer. Rock piles and scree slopes provide homes for hoary marmots whose whistles echo from mountainside to mountainside. A rare grapefern also occurs in the alpine zone. Rabbit-like pikas are found on high, wind-swept slopes where delicate white mountain avens, cinquefoils, alpine forget-me-nots, saxifrages, the exquisite grass-of-Parnassus, stonecrop and moss campion grow. Here, water pipits, horned larks and white-tailed ptarmigan can nest in relative isolation. The gray-crowned rosy finch may also be spotted nesting in a jumble of boulders or in a niche on a rock face.

The fairly pure stand of alpine larch underlain with grouseberry and wild strawberry which occurs on the northwest face of Beehive Mountain is a fairly uncommon sight in the Alberta Rockies. Some towering old fire-kill snags and the strewn deadfall of a once mature forest above treeline on Beehive may well indicate that extensive alpine larch stands previously occurred here.

The historic Tornado Pass area contains a very rich subalpine meadow harbouring many examples of flora common to more southerly regions. So profuse are its flowers that it was under consideration by the Alberta government as a Natural Area.

The Upper Oldman contains significant habitat for bighorn sheep, grizzly bears and elk. One of the largest elk herds in southern Alberta, numbering 400-500 animals, returns from winter grazing areas in the Whaleback to the east of the Upper Oldman to calve. With their offspring,

LEFT: *Sparkling waters flow through dense, cool, old growth forests.* ABOVE: *Windblown limber pine on Cabin Ridge.*

they later move from the valley floor of the Oldman River up to the open slopes and ridges at higher elevations for summer grazing. Mineral licks and dirt wallows are scattered throughout the area. Some particularly large ones are located within the Hidden Creek sub-basin, along Soda Creek and up on the slopes of Beehive Mountain. The fall rut occurs in the Upper Oldman before the elk herds once again move back to their winter ranges.

The relatively undisturbed nature of the Upper Oldman provides excellent habitat for grizzly bears, with around nine of these masters of the wilderness using the Upper Oldman and adjacent areas across the Continental Divide into British Columbia. Good summer habitat is used by black bears in the lower valleys.

Bighorn sheep herds also summer in the proposed Upper Oldman Wildland Recreation Areas. These herds move through Windy Pass into British Columbia or across the Oldman River Valley to winter on the chinook-cleared slopes of Pasque Mountain and Cabin Ridge. Scattered groups of mountain goats seldom stray from the security of their rocky ledges on the Continental Divide.

The Oldman River, including its length through the proposed Wildland Recreation Area, is an outstanding fishery, one of Alberta's few Class I trout fisheries. The headwaters of the Oldman and tributaries such as Hidden Creek are key to this fishery because they provide the brood-rearing habitat for bull trout and Rocky Mountain whitefish. Pools in the streams also provide the overwintering habitat for these native populations. Cutthroat trout and bull trout inhabit Hidden Creek. Our native cutthroat also occurs in Oyster, Slacker and Straight creeks. Cutthroat, rainbow, bull trout and Rocky Mountain whitefish live in the Oldman River. Eastern brook trout have been introduced into Lost and Cummings creeks.

Recognizing the natural quality and expanse of alpine and subalpine plant and animal communities in the Upper Oldman, the Alberta government has been considering protecting a small area centred around Beehive Mountain as a Natural Area.

Recreation

The Upper Oldman has been a popular destination for southern Albertans for the last 30 years. Thousands of people now visit the watershed areas during July and August.

For the hiker, horseback rider, hunter or fisherman, the Upper Oldman Wildland Recreation Area, in all its moods, offers a range of rich experiences. Forming the eastern boundary of the proposed area, the Oldman River cascades over a set of dramatic falls and weaves through tranquil deep pools shaded by willows. The variety of excellent habitats created by this river and its tributaries hosts populations of native sport fish. Cutthroat and bull trout, rainbow trout and Rocky Mountain whitefish are found in this Class I watershed. In the 1920s, outfitters were successful in getting the Forest Service to put a stop to settlers from the Cardston area who annually pickled and dried fish on the Oldman River, hauling the fish out by the wagonload. Since 1978, easy motorized access to the river has once again depleted this resource,

lowering the success rate of fishing and reducing the average size of the fish. Fortunately, the wilderness beauty of this fisherman's paradise helps compensate for poor fish yields. Fishing is now only open in alternate years in order to try and protect this natural fishery.

The Oldman River from its origin in a small alpine tarn on Mount Lyall to the North Fork bridge several kilometres downstream of the proposed Upper Oldman Wildland Recreation Area has been designated for protection by the Alberta Wilderness Association as a candidate "recreational river". Its spectacular scenery, fishing, wildlife and river-based recreation were the assets contributing to its designation (for more information see the book *Rivers on Borrowed Time*). Whitewater canoeing and kayaking usually occur from late April until about the end of June, depending on the water levels.

Spectacular populations of elk, mule deer, moose, grizzlies and trophy bighorn rams have lured hunters and outfitters into the area since 1915.

Because the Upper Oldman, and indeed the whole watershed, is quite narrow, the area can be traversed widthwise in a single day's round trip by horse or foot from the road along the Oldman River. The only exception to this is the Hidden Creek sub-basin, which is ideal for an overnight trip. Those seeking more extensive trips can find highly scenic routes running the length of the Continental Divide within the Upper Oldman or can make use of Northfork, Tornado and Windy passes which lead into British Columbia. Seven different access trails up creek valleys onto the Divide provide ample opportunities for looped trips. The Great Divide Trail System, developed by volunteers, runs along the Continental Divide from Lost Creek in the north to North Fork Pass in the south, and incorporates many of the traditional horse and foot trails.

Whatever route the traveller chooses, a few hours of travel will bring visitors to the breathtaking wilderness views the Upper Oldman is famous for. The broad valley of the Oldman River sweeps up through deep green forests patterned by past fires and onto open alpine slopes and rugged peaks which march off as far as the eye can see to the north and south. To the east are the open grassy slopes and limber pine ridges of Pasque Mountain and Cabin Ridge, with the grey rock of the Livingstone Range towering behind. Seismic lines and old pack trails onto the Pasque Mountain/Cabin Ridge complex provide access to the lengthy ridge walks or rides which can be taken in full view of the splendour of the Upper Oldman Wildland to the west.

The Upper Oldman also has peaks, such as

There are many excellent locations for bull trout in the Upper Oldman Wildland Recreation Area.

Tornado Mountain, the Gauntlet and Mount Lyall, which are popular climbing destinations. Tornado Mountain was picked as one of 75 Alberta peaks on which a climbing cairn was placed during Alberta's 75th Anniversary.

The Upper Oldman's deep snowfall, valley trails and open forests provide good backcountry skiing and snowshoeing opportunities, although its cross-country skiing qualities seem only to be realized by local residents. Since the advent of snowmobiling, it has also been one of the popular snowmobiling areas, with snowmobile use usually concentrated along the Oldman River.

Access

Most visitors reach the Upper Oldman via the road which runs along the Oldman River northwest off the Forestry Trunk Road (Highway 940). Both a group camp complete with corrals, and a public campground are located near the road junction. However, many prefer to random camp or make their staging area in one of the more than 100 sites along the Oldman River road.

The Upper Oldman can also be entered from the north by horse or foot along the Cataract Creek logging road (closed to motorized use) and south along the Great Divide Trail from Lost Creek.

North Fork Pass, the lush subalpine meadows of Tornado Pass and the notch between Tornado and Gould Dome which leads into the head of South Hidden Creek can all be reached by driving up a logging road, the Atlas Road, from

Allison Creek north of Coleman. Road conditions should be checked with the **Alberta Forest Service** office in Blairmore before beginning a trip.

Several guides use the Upper Oldman area, and this wilderness is used regularly by at least three commercial outfitters.

Land Use Concerns and Recommendations

In the narrow southern region of the Eastern Slopes where intensive resource activities such as logging and coal mining have been going on since the early 1900s, the fact that the lands of the Upper Oldman have remained intact for so long is attributable to a combination of the poor quality of its timber and minerals and the high cost of removing some of its resources such as coal.

Despite the Upper Oldman's many wilderness attributes and its popularity for recreation, only the mountain peaks and alpine areas above 1980 metres have any type of protection. Even at that, this quasi-protection is only in the form of a policy which has zoned these high elevation lands as Prime Protection. A 62 square kilometre area centred around Beehive Mountain has been under consideration by the government since the early 1970s as a potential Natural Area. The remainder of the proposed Upper Oldman Wildland Recreation Area has been zoned as Multiple Use, which would allow the full range of resource developments to go ahead.

Although the Pasque/Cabin Ridge complex

which forms the eastern half of the Upper Oldman watershed is not within the proposed Wildland Recreation Area, these Chinook-blown landscapes deserve protection for their scenic and wildlife values. The boundaries of the proposed Upper Oldman Wildland Recreation Area have been drawn to allow for continued motorized use and random camping along the eastward side of the Oldman River. However, any visitor to the area has a view of this whole narrow watershed. The very scenic natural viewscape of this popular recreation area should be kept intact. The critical wildlife habitat of this ridge complex also warrants careful protective management.

While the natural beauty of the Upper Oldman should be reason enough to ensure its protection, it is also important to note that its preservation would yield economic benefits. Tourism and recreation are important industries in Alberta, and they will become particularly important in southwestern Alberta as mature forests and markets for coal and timber dwindle. The value of pristine landscapes and preserved wildlife habitats can be computed in economic terms as well as social terms.

Logging

In 1974, a logging licence was established on the Oyster, Pasque and Straight Creek drainages. The licence was issued before a decision was made based on the recommendations coming from the 1973 public hearings on the Eastern Slopes held by the Environment Conservation Authority; the licence has continued to this day. It was originally expected that the timber would

be cut in 1977-78, but no timber has yet been cut from the licence area. In 1984, the company holding the licence closed its sawmill.

Despite comprehensive government resource studies which specifically concluded that Hidden Creek, the largest sub-basin of the Upper Oldman watershed, should not be logged due to watershed and fishing concerns as well as its steep terrain, a logging licence was issued in 1980. Final approval to log this subalpine forest in the heart of the proposed Wildland Recreation Area was given by the Minister responsible for the Forest Service in November of 1983. However, as of December 1985, only one-fifth of the necessary logging haul road has been built and no cutting has taken place due to a slump in the lumber market. While allowing for streamside buffers, and no cutting on slopes over 30 degrees, the harvesting program is to remove all merchantable timber from the area below the 1982 metre elevation line in two passes of logging, spaced 20 years apart. The first pass involves clearcuts totalling about 880 hectares of the merchantable timber located in the headwaters of Hidden Creek.

Due to the poor economics associated with logging the area and the recently documented high recreation value of the area, the Alberta Wilderness Association still holds out hope for saving these wilderness lands from disturbance.

Taking a rest stop below Beehive peak. A well known local landmark, this mountain with its expansive alpine meadows is at the heart of the provincial government's proposed Beehive Mountain Natural Area.

Oil, Gas and Coal

The first exploration well to be approved in the Upper Oldman area was given the go-ahead in 1977. It was a decision that met with much opposition from conservationists, for the location approved was at the headwaters of the Oldman River, less than a kilometre inside the government's proposed Natural Area. The well was dry, but the 29 kilometre road constructed along the old cart trail running the length of the Oldman River has resulted in today's problems with random motorized use, and the intensive hunting and fishing pressure.

Petroleum and natural gas leases still cover substantial portions of the Upper Oldman, but to date, exploration through two additional wells just to the east of the proposed Wildland Recreation Area and seismic lines throughout have not turned up any economical gas reserves. The most recent well was drilled at 2256 metres elevation on Pasque Mountain within lands zoned as Critical Wildlife. These lands are critical bighorn sheep winter range.

Although seismic lines and well access roads in the Upper Oldman have been reclaimed, off-road vehicle use, which is permitted throughout the entire watershed, has laid the reclamation to waste.

Coal leases extend over the Pasque Mountain/Cabin Ridge complex across the Oldman River from the proposed Wildland Recreation Area. The majority of the Upper Oldman Wildland is placed off-limits to coal development by the Coal Policy. At present, development of the Pasque/Cabin Ridge complex is unlikely as most of the area is zoned under the Eastern Slopes Policy as Critical Wildlife.

Minerals

There are traces of lead, zinc and silver in the Mount Gass area. Reportedly, there is not enough ore to make these deposits economical for development. However, applications have again been made to carry out exploration in the Mount Gass area.

Off-Road Vehicle Use

Seismic lines extend up seven creek valleys in the Upper Oldman. As well, there is a network of traditional foot and horse trails through the high country. Because of the open nature of the alpine area and some of the forests, all of these routes are extensively travelled by off-road vehicles, particularly trail bikes and all-terrain vehicles. Such uncontrolled use is causing extensive damage to the sensitive alpine and subalpine vegetation, to horse/foot trails and to wildlife and fisheries habitat. In the interest of protecting the many natural resources of these high mountain landscapes, motorized use should be restricted to the road and random campsites along the Oldman River.

Grazing

Due to government policies at the time, overgrazing was a problem prior to the 1950s. Upper reaches of the Upper Oldman area have since recovered, but range conditions for grazing are still only rated as fair to poor. Since 1974, some segments have often been closed to domestic grazing.

North Porcupine Hills
A Rich Mosaic

The coffee cup warmed numb fingers as the dawn approached. To the east, the hills were stark silhouettes with the sunrise turning clouds a vivid red. In the darkness of the valley below the ridge, an elk barked.

With every passing moment, I was more convinced my plan would work. I had hiked along the ridge the night before, sleeping in a small depression. Curling up on a cushion of bunchgrass, I had only a gnarled old willow for company. Brushing the frost off my pack, I reach for a cranberry-stained sandwich.

The light grew stronger. Carefully wiping frost from the rifle, I left the newly purchased scope covers in place to prevent unnecessary fogging. My plan depended upon other hunters walking into the valley at first light. Last season I had joined these hunters as we flushed the elk herd through a narrow gap in the ridge above. The gnarled old willow beside me today was in that gap.

Suddenly, a cow elk appeared at the edge of the gap, then another and another. Not in a hurry, the cows even paused to graze on the bunchgrasses. Slowly they passed within 50 metres. The air was calm, no drifting scent would alarm the elk.

Another cow appeared. The herd was coming now. I placed one hand on the rifle beside me. There was a spike bull on my side of the herd. I'd wait until he was opposite. Slowly they moved forward. Elk at the rear of the herd kept looking back. Hunters coming into the valley below were doing their job.

My hands started to shake. The spike bull would pass within 30 metres. A clear shot. I tensed, and then the white-tipped antlers of a herd bull came into view over the ridge. The big bull dwarfed a four point that accompanied him. *"Don't move a muscle,"* I told myself. Five hundred metres, 400, 350 metres - I had paced off all the distances the evening before.

A shot rang out from the valley below.

The herd ran by on a dead run. The big bull ran directly toward me, followed by a four point. As he approached within a stone's throw, I grabbed the rifle and swung it to my shoulder. *The scope caps. I had forgotten to remove the scope caps.* The thunder of their hooves was deafening as they passed by. Frantically, I ripped off the scope caps and swung the rifle barrel ahead of the big bull. The four point moved in beside him. Then they were in the trees, gone.

Perhaps some plans are never made to work.

I n 1872, Colonel Robertson-Ross, Commanding Officer of the Canadian Militia, was dispatched to western Canada to investigate stories of lawlessness among white traders, Indians and new settlers.

Like many before him, Robertson-Ross travelled down the valley between the Porcupine Hills and the Livingstone Range, en route to North Kootenay Pass. Upon reaching the North Porcupine Hills area, a violent snow storm kept the party snow-bound for six days. On September 26th, the Colonel rode to the top of the Hills. Obviously impressed by the scene before him, he wrote:

I had I think, one of the most magnificent views I ever saw in my life. At a distance varying from 15 to 20 miles, in a sort of immense amphitheatre lay the Rocky Mountains, towering their giant heads many thousands of feet high; on our left the boundless prairie stretching far to the east; in our front to the south at a distance of 50 or 60 miles the boundary line, the Chief Mountain, and part of the Territory of Montana.

The Colonel's vantage point had been named "Ky-es-kaghp-ogh-suy-iss"or porcupine's tail by

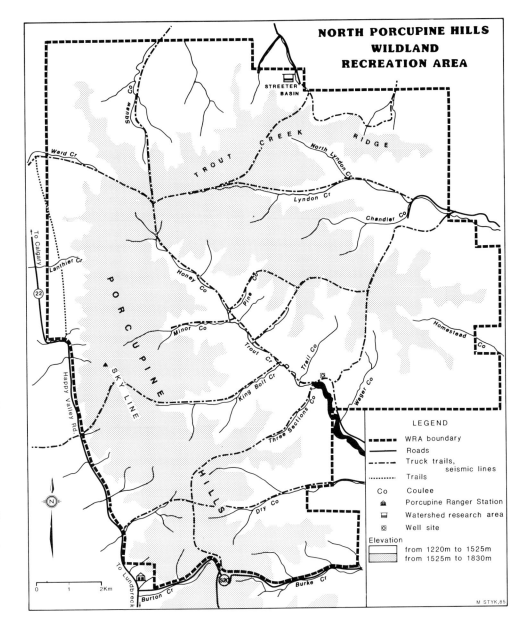

NORTH PORCUPINE HILLS WILDLAND RECREATION AREA

LEGEND
- - - - WRA boundary
——— Roads
-·-·- Truck trails, seismic lines
········ Trails
Co   Coulee
🏠 Porcupine Ranger Station
⊟ Watershed research area
◉ Well site

Elevation
▢ from 1220m to 1525m
▨ from 1525m to 1830m

M STYK,85

Peigan Indians for the tapering silhouette of hills bristling with Douglas fir and limber pine.

The gentle, rounded hills, deep coulees and rugged west escarpment of the Porcupine Hills stand between the Rockies and prairies, yet belong to neither. Though geographically part of the foothills, the Porcupine Hills are geologically unique and distinct from the "true" foothills.

In the central portion of this formation, 130 square kilometres has been selected by the AWA as a proposed Wildland Recreation Area. In its relatively small area the North Porcupine Hills Wildland contains a rich mosaic of five distinct vegetation types: the montane forest of the chinook-dominated southwest, the subalpine forest of the mountains lying to the west, the aspen parkland of central Alberta, the boreal forest of the north and the grasslands of the prairies to the east. Nowhere else in Alberta do these vegetation types co-exist in such a small area. In winter, chinook winds modify the climate and contribute to the area's importance as winter habitat for elk, moose and deer.

In summer and fall, the North Porcupine Hills are used extensively for cattle grazing, hunting, hiking, horse packing and primitive camping. The region's biological diversity, history, recreational potential and proximity to the major centres of Calgary and Lethbridge have prompted the selection of the North Porcupine Hills as a Wildland Recreation Area. It is important to protect this public land from development so that future generations may enjoy its diversity and delight in its natural charm, as did Colonel Robertson-Ross over one hundred years ago.

A gnarled limber pine clinging to life along the Skyline.

Geological History

Although the Porcupine Hills at first glance appear to be part of the foothills to their west, their structure is notably different. Like most of the Eastern Slopes, the Porcupine Hills were elevated during underground disturbances which produced the Rocky Mountains and foothills. However, unlike the dramatically folded and faulted rock of the foothills and mountains, the Porcupine Hills are a large block of sandstone and shale gently tilted to the east. With their high western escarpment and gentle eastward-dipping beds of rock laid down by ancient freshwater lakes and rivers, the Hills are structurally more akin to the plains. The western edge of the North Porcupine Hills or "Skyline", with its highest point at 1583 meters, forms the western edge of the Alberta Syncline.

At least twice, major ice sheets moved through the area, carving long, flat valleys and graceful coulees. During the last continental glaciation, the ice mass moved into, around and through the Hills from the north, east and south with a glacial tongue wedging up the valley of Trout Creek. Unlike the major portion of Alberta, the Wildland Recreation Area lands above 1615 metres were generally left untouched by the last glaciation.

Human History

The gentle terrain of the North Porcupine Hills has, for hundreds of years, sustained Blackfoot and Peigan Indian hunters who killed buffalo by driving them over steep coulees in the area. There are several unnamed jumps in the North Porcupine Hills region where elk and bison bones have been found.

The Peigan Indians came west to the Hills to escape harsh winters and food scarcities on the prairies. Occasionally, to increase game habitat, Indian peoples burned brush and trees, which in turn encouraged grassland growth for grazing wildlife. This practice, in addition to natural fires, had affected vegetation before explorers like John Palliser visited the Porcupine Hills in 1858. Effective fire suppression in recent times has reduced the grassland and the Douglas fir savannahs.

The relatively flat landscape flanking the Hills was travelled often. Stoney, Kootenay and Flathead peoples used the Stoney Trail through the broad valley on the west side parallel to the Porcupine Hills, while pioneers, missionaries, whisky traders and the Northwest Mounted Police travelled the east side of the Porcupine Hills to get from Fort Macleod to Fort Calgary. This route today is Highway 2.

Whisky traders who had posts throughout the region during the 1870s sometimes hid in the Hills to avoid the Northwest Mounted Police. Of the some 26 small whisky trading posts eventually built, one was on Willow Creek in the Porcupine Hills just to the north of the Wildland Recreation Area. When a Northwest Mounted Police post was established at High River to the northeast, the Hills were patrolled more often and ceased to harbor the traders.

By 1880, the bison which used to winter in the Porcupine Hills were exterminated, and the Peigan people were living on a reserve at the southern end of the Hills. Shortly thereafter, the Dominion government began to lease the Porcupine Hills and surrounding lands for cattle grazing. Huge cattle herds were brought in from Montana and leases were granted for 21 years at an annual rental of one dollar per acre. This now was cattle country, and the ranching business thrived as cattlemen were called on to supply Canadian Pacific Railway construction crews and treaty Indians who could no longer survive on the diminishing wild game populations.

Until 1950, it was government policy to allow heavy grazing in the belief that this would reduce the hazard of wildfire. Such a heavy-handed practice took its toll on the wildlife, watershed and native grasslands of the Hills.

Vegetation

As unique as its geology, the vegetation of the North Porcupine Hills is a complex mosaic of five distinct vegetation types: montane forests dominated by Douglas fir, subalpine forests composed of Engelmann spruce, white spruce of the boreal forest, aspen parkland and fescue grasslands. Within these diverse wilderness lands are the largest recorded Douglas fir trees in Alberta; many of these monarchs are over 400 years old and up to 1.2 metres in diametre.

Extensive stands of Douglas fir with limber pine along exposed ridges characterize the montane zone. Douglas fir are most predominant on high, dry, south-facing slopes. Found on North America's west coast and as far south as California, Douglas fir forests occur only in isolated patches in southern Alberta. In the proposed Wildland Recreation Area many of these magnificent trees, with their thick, fire-resistant bark, have grown to heights of 26 metres. The common ground fires of the past helped maintain the open grass understory of the Douglas fir savannahs. Douglas fir are also found mixed with lodgepole pine and spruce on north-facing slopes, towering above the other conifers. Gnarled old limber pine are a distinctive feature of many of the rocky, wind-blown ridges of the North Porcupine Hills where the environment is too harsh for other trees.

Aged stands of tall, white spruce, draped with lichen beards and located in moist shady hollows, have managed to survive the many fires that used to sweep the area. White and Engelmann spruce prefer the shadier, cooler areas. These trees,

mingled with Douglas fir on north-facing slopes, provide ideal conditions for an understory of white meadowsweet, heart-leaved arnica, grouse-berry and bunchberry.

Lodgepole pine have responded in the wake of fire, growing to impressive heights on dry, sunny slopes with an understory of white meadowsweet, fireweed and wild rose. Covering much of western North America, lodgepole pine is one of the first trees to grow after a burn because of its resinous cones which resist destruction and its tolerance of direct sunlight. Although in 1919 a forest fire burned 2500 hectares in the Porcupine Hills, most fires have been successfully suppressed since the Porcupine Hills were incorporated into the Forest Reserve in 1912, with the result that the natural vegetation pattern has been upset. The long absence of wildfire has allowed aspen to invade the grasslands and has encouraged the growth of saplings and shrubs in the Douglas fir savannahs. Thus, once abundant, the Douglas fir savannahs are now rare in the Hills.

In the North Porcupine Hills, aspen poplar once contained by frequent fires now dominate valley bottoms, and mingle with grasslands on dry slopes and with conifers on well drained sites. Plants and flowers typical of the aspen parkland include wild onion, prairie crocus, shooting star, loco-weed and patches of Saskatoon bushes. Water birch, willow, marsh reed grass, cow parsnip and larkspur, a plant poisonous to cattle, grow along streams.

LEFT: *The Columbian ground squirrel, an inquisitive mountain rodent found throughout the mountainous areas of Alberta.*

Wildlife and Fish

The diversity of vegetation in the North Porcupine Hills provides bountiful food and shelter for deer, moose, elk, coyotes, snowshoe hares, black bears, lynx and cougars. A small herd of elk, along with deer and moose, inhabit the North Porcupine Hills year-round. In fall, elk from the mountains in the west migrate to forage in the warmth and shelter of their winter ranges in the Hills.

The strong chinook winds and solar heat expose forage on the south- and west-facing slopes. Recent studies show a relatively high average concentration of about one moose per square kilometre in the area. Along with mule deer, the moose favor the willow-covered flats along streams.

The diverse vegetation and terrain provides the habitat most sought by cougars. Rock outcrops of the North Porcupines are favourite denning and hunting sites for the significant cougar population. The actual size of the population, though, has not been determined. Black bears and wolves also live in the proposed Wildland Recreation Area. However, there have been no recent grizzly sightings. Small mammals like the Columbian ground squirrel are abundant in open grasslands and herb meadows.

The diversity of the vegetation is also reflected in the variety of birds which can be observed in the area. For example, the lazuli bunting which inhabits deciduous woods and the Cassin's finch which inhabits coniferous and mixed-wood forests of the southern mountains both live in the North Porcupines. Blue grouse of the subalpine forests and Douglas fir stands, rough grouse of the aspen parkland and spruce grouse of the white spruce and lodgepole pine forests are all present.

Broad fluctuations and generally low summer water levels combined with siltation and pollution from cattle and their wastes inhibit fish populations in the streams. Trout Creek and Lyndon Creek are the only permanent creeks which contain sport fish.

Recreation

The North Porcupine Hills present recreational opportunities for southern Alberta residents seeking wilderness solitude close to home. The area is less than a two hour drive from Calgary or Lethbridge and its gentle, scenic hills can be enjoyed by hikers, backpackers and horseback riders of all fitness and skill levels. Some trails climb to views above 1525 metres along the western edge of the Skyline or on the ridge between the Trout Creek and Lyndon Creek basins, while others meander in leisurely fashion through coulees.

There is many a local southern Albertan who will take a day-trip up along the Skyline to view the unmarred expanses of the Whaleback, the Livingstone Range and the peaks of the Continental Divide to the west. The distinguishing eye can see the Livingstone Range and behind it, Tornado Mountain and Beehive Mountain, part of the chain of Continental Divide peaks within the proposed Upper Oldman Wildland Recreation Area.

For the traveller, the North Porcupines present a self-contained wilderness composed largely of the Trout Creek drainage. Standing in the valley of Trout Creek, the visitor is presented with a natural tapestry of vegetation and terrain and is totally unaware of the surrounding settled lands. Travellers should bring a compass, topographic map and, if travelling later in the summer, water. Many of the hills and coulees may appear similar in appearance to the newcomer, making it easy to become lost. As well, many of the creeks and streams are dry in summer.

Old cart trails which lead up almost every coulee and the gentle open terrain allow easy travel by horse or foot. Trout Creek basin and surrounding ridges, such as the Skyline along the western escarpment, are key routes for refreshing spring trips and impressive views of prairie and mountain landscapes.

In late spring and early summer, while the mountains to the west are still under snow, visitors are rewarded by the multitude of wild flowers and the pleasant climate of the North Porcupines. A combination of scant snowfall (only 20 centimetres average from October to April) and chinook winds often free the southerly facing hills of snow during the winter. Snow is gone from the North Porcupines by March. When there is snow, the North Porcupine Hills can provide snowshoeing experiences or exciting cross-country skiing with their many long open runs.

Many areas are ideal for berry picking and wildlife watching. The diversity and range of plant communities in the North Porcupine Hills invites exploration. With this wilderness's past history of fires and grazing, one can easily observe patterns of plant succession.

Hunting and Fishing

Fishing is generally fair but only in streams which have been stocked. Lyndon Creek and Trout Creek are stocked annually with rainbow trout, but most other streams dry up during the summer. This wilderness area is popular among hunters seeking deer, moose, elk, black bear and upland game birds. Recently, bow hunting has become a very popular pursuit in the Hills.

Access

There are a number of options for starting points for trips into the North Porcupines, with the undeveloped staging area on secondary road 520, (Burke Creek Road) where it crosses the top of the Skyline being the most popular. The visitor could also begin trips from Highway 22 (Happy Valley Road), off the South Willow Creek Road, or from the road leading partway up Lyndon Creek. Another popular access point is from the road off the 520 leading up Trout Creek on the southeast side of the Hills.

Once the Trout Creek basin in the heart of the North Porcupines is entered, the overnight traveller has a number of looped route options which include sections of the Skyline. Another highly recommended destination is attained by travelling northeast from Trout Creek to Lyndon Creek. Views from the 1770-metre ridge dividing these two watersheds will reveal a remote corner of this wilderness dominated by an intricate series of ridges and hills.

Land Use Concerns and Recommendations

The proposed North Porcupine Wildland Recreation Area is within the Forest Reserve and falls under the jurisdiction of the Alberta Forest Service. Although it is widely recognized by southern Albertans for its natural beauty, wildlife populations and recreational opportunities, much of the area is under lease for natural gas, petroleum and coal exploration, as well as logging and grazing. Since 1977, all of the area with the exception of a small Critical Wildlife Zone in the southeast has been zoned Multiple Use under the Eastern Slopes Policy.

As is common with most of the Eastern Slopes, motorized use is not controlled within the Porcupine Hills. With the many gentle access routes to the North Porcupine Hills and the old cart trails leading up most coulees, motorized use by all types of vehicles is a serious environmental problem throughout these wilderness lands.

Grazing

Cattle grazing is the oldest land use in the North Porcupine Hills. Three grazing allotments encompass the North Porcupine Hills. The number of cattle grazed on each allotment is now carefully controlled by the government and there appears to be adequate forage for both cattle and wildlife in the Wildland Recreation Area. Water siltation can occur where cattle trample streambeds. However, cattle grazing overall is compatible with the goals of wilderness recreation, providing it is carefully managed so that the fisheries and winter food supplies for wildlife are not threatened. Indeed, with the demise of the bison, grazing has become a necessary management tool for maintaining the natural diversity of grassland plants.

In the interest of maintaining the variety of distinct vegetation types which historically were kept intact by re-occurring wildfires, a wise management plan for the North Porcupine Hills should include controlled burning to simulate that fire history. In turn, this will aid in the maintenance and development of the grasslands needed for both wildlife and cattle.

Logging

Since the early 1900s, settlers have selectively removed timber from the area for homes and ranch buildings. As of 1980, the Alberta Forest Services policy for the North Porcupine Hills is to allow 50 percent removal of all merchantable trees in the North Porcupines, with the exception of the very old Douglas fir stands. This is to be done through annual clearing of a total of just over 20 hectares of forest. This clearcut logging program begun in 1981 is scheduled to complete the 50 percent removal by 1991. The adjacent "reserve" stands of trees, the remaining 50 percent, would be cut when the first cut-over areas have regenerated to trees two metres high or when 20 years have passed. However, with the economic slump in the lumber market, cutting has often been suspended. Selective sanitation logging has been conducted to remove trees infested with mountain pine beetle.

Oil, Gas and Coal

Most of the North Porcupine Hills are under oil and gas lease, and one well was drilled in 1981 on the east side of Trout Creek Basin between Wager and Trail coulees. Douglas fir trees over 400 years old were felled along the Skyline for the sake of widening and upgrading the old cart trail into an access road for the drilling rig. This 10 kilometre access road, which was then cut along the graceful Three Sections Coulee, ended at the drilling site a mere 200 metres away from an existing valley bottom road entering from the southeast along Trout Creek. In all, a heart-breaking and needless marring of this wilderness landscape. Drilling, completed in 1982, appears of dubious economic success. In 1985, conservationists were still pressing for full reclamation of the access road and well site.

Coal

The Coal Policy of 1976 has zoned the entire North Porcupines as Category III, allowing for coal exploration and development where development of the necessary mining infrastructure, such as a community for the employees, is determined to be in the public's interest. To date, there has been very little interest in coal exploration in the area. Cursory exploration has only indicated some small coal seams.

The Whaleback
Chinook Wind and Douglas Fir Kaleidoscope

The late autumn and early spring are periods of relative inactivity for many outdoor enthusiasts. The trails in the "real mountains" are covered with too much snow to allow enjoyable hiking, yet the snowpack is either too shallow or rotten to be worth skiing. In the autumn, water is scarce and the area is actively being hunted, so it is especially in the spring that I turn my attention to the foothills of southern Alberta.

One of the most rewarding foothills hikes is the Whaleback Ridge, located approximately 140 kilometres south of Calgary along Highway 22. Looking much like a gigantic beached whale from the air, this ridge stretches north for some 30 kilometres from its southern tip on the banks of the Oldman River.

Although Highway 22 from Longview to Lundbreck provides easy access to the Whaleback Ridge from the east side, the five-to-nine kilometres of distance and a series of low intervening ridges serve to visually isolate the main ridge.

The access to the south end is easy via a grazing co-operative road along the north side of the Oldman River. Most day trips start at this end. Access to the north end, for those interested in a two-to-four day traverse of the ridge, is via a short farm road spur off the Chaffen road. About half the ridge is leased rangeland. The western parts of it that fall within the Bow-Crow Forest Reserve are also leased under grazing permits to local ranches.

At its southern terminus near the Oldman

The Anise Swallowtail inhabits river bottom areas in the aspen parklands of south-central Alberta and occasionally travels to the foothills and front ranges of the Eastern Slopes.

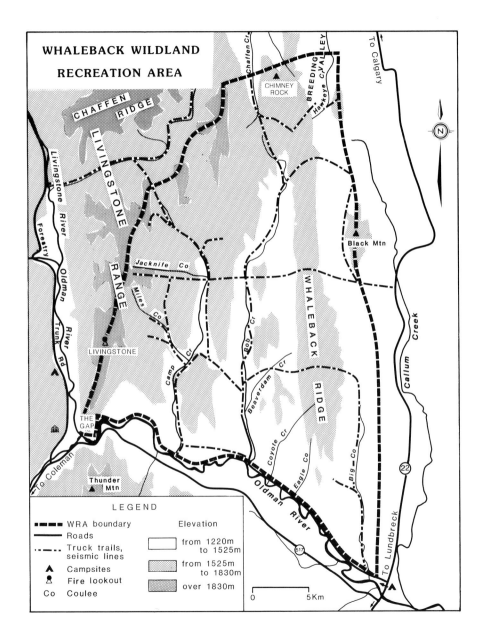

River, the elevation of the surrounding prairie is about 1210 metres. From here the ridge quickly climbs to just over 1525 metres, and after eight kilometres reaches its highest point of 1784 metres. At first glance, these elevation figures may seem rather trivial, but when all the ups and downs are added up, it turns out that there are over 3050 metres of elevation gains and losses.

Route finding on the Whaleback is often a simple matter of sticking to the ridge top. In many cases, however, animal trails will traverse neatly around a peak or rocky area. As a general rule, these animal routes make for much easier hiking and often lead to some very interesting spots.

For example, on the first half of the ridge, water is in short supply as there are no clean streams or springs. After 15 kilometres, there is a bit of a kink in the ridgeline, and instead of following the crest, the trail shortcuts the bend, only to emerge from a lovely section of forest at the site of a clear, cold spring. This happens again several times along the ridge.

The vegetation varies a great deal from the south to the north along the ridge. The south end is quite dry and open. The only trees in this section are gnarled old limber pines, which cling tenaciously to tiny rock outcrops.

Farther along the ridge, the cooler, moister north-facing slopes begin to contain pockets of spruce, while the wind-protected but sunny southeast slopes harbour groves of stately Douglas firs.

At the half-way point, entire slopes are carpeted with a quiltwork of spruce, aspen and pine, while the trees on the ridge crest become more dense and less gnarled.

Eventually at the extreme northern end of the Whaleback, the forest cover of mature spruce and patches of aspen is broken only by the occasional meadow.

Flowers, which have yet to emerge from beneath the mountain snowpack, are already in full bloom on the Whaleback. Prairie crocuses, wood lilies, shooting stars, forget-me-nots and even glacier lilies all appear here months ahead of their mountain cousins.

Wildlife is abundant and varied here, particularly in the springtime. I've seen elk, moose, coyote, black bear and over 100 deer on a single weekend outing.

One of the attractions of any ridge walk is the 360° view of the surrounding topography. Due to the geographical location of the Whaleback Ridge, the views along its crest are most impressive and varied.

To the west, one overlooks the entire Livingstone Range and beyond it, the High Rock Range summits of the Continental Divide. To the south lies the broad prairie land of southern Alberta, with the peaks of Glacier Park, Montana and Waterton forming the backdrop. The Porcupine Hills dominate the eastern horizon and countless rows of foothills to the north complete the scene.

It could be that the dramatic splendour of massive mountain faces have blinded our ability to see the more subtle beauty of less rugged terrain. Or perhaps the foothills are ignored because they have not been identified as "wild" by government statute – the old "if it's not park, its not wilderness" attitude. A trip in the Whaleback will quickly put this myth to rest.

The smooth, rounded hills of the Whaleback Ridge rise from the landscape like the vertebrae of a humpback whale. Once, Indian hunters gazed from atop the 1800 metre ridge over grassy hillsides and broad valleys dotted with buffalo, and explorers used this landmark to guide them in their travels.

The spectacular, full circle view from the Whaleback Ridge has changed little over the years, with the foothills and rugged Rocky Mountain peaks to the west, and the Porcupine Hills and sunlit prairie beyond to the east. Of course now there are more settlements and roads, but being ranching country, the wild character of the land has remained for the most part. The Whaleback is only 140 kilometres south of Calgary, just west of Highway 22. A 500 kilovolt powerline has been constructed along its east side and cattle have replaced the buffalo.

The Whaleback Ridge is the focal landmark in a 236 square kilometre parcel of folded ridges proposed as the Whaleback Wildland Recreation Area. The Whaleback has a kaleidoscope of unique features; the vegetation, wildlife, and landforms of this wilderness make it one of the most diverse in Alberta.

The Whaleback is the largest relatively undisturbed tract of montane landscape in Canada. Warmed by the chinook winds, this highly scenic area is characterized by grassland, yielding to open stands of Douglas fir and limber pine. Montane environments are common within the Rocky Mountain region of the northwestern United States and the warm, dry regions of southern Alberta and British Columbia. Most of these areas, however, have been disrupted by logging or damaged by overgrazing.

Landscapes include almost every conceivable montane vegetation type, with the exception of ponderosa pine. Visitors to the Whaleback can explore marshes and grasslands, lush meadows, Douglas fir savannahs and barren mountain peaks. This magnificent diversity encourages equally diverse animal life. This wilderness is a sanctuary for mountain lions, golden eagles and grizzly bears, all of which prefer vast, undisturbed territory in which to live. About 1,300 elk winter among the warm, chinook-cleared hills of the Whaleback area, making it, along with the Panther Corners area, one of Alberta's two most important winter ranges for elk.

The Whaleback's wilderness is also a sanctuary for people. Its flowing ridges are accessible year-round to backcountry travellers. It is popular among hikers, horseback riders and fall sportsmen. With its complex geological origins and interesting human history, the Whaleback provides a bridge to our ancient and recent past.

Aside from ranching, no human settlement exists in the Whaleback, as the majority of the area lies within the Forest Reserve; these are public lands reserved from settlement. Much of the Whaleback is, however, leased for cattle grazing, which, if undertaken properly, is a land use compatible with wilderness management.

The Alberta Wilderness Association is striving to preserve the Whaleback wilderness so it may continue as a sanctuary for wildlife and a refuge for people.

Geological History

Many millions of years ago, great slabs of rock were moved east and northeast along the Livingstone Thrust Fault, which aligns along Camp Creek, pushing older rock over much younger strata. This rock formed the Livingstone Range on the western boundary of the Wildland Recreation Area. Part of the front range of the Rocky Mountains, this range rises to a height of up to 2180 metres at its crest. The Livingstone formation is built of sandstones, conglomerates and carbonaceous shale, with coal outcrops at the base of the Range.

To the east of the Livingstone Range lie a complex series of dramatically faulted and folded ridges. The best example of these ridges is the Whaleback. The Whaleback is a west-dipping thrust fault which extends from the Oldman River north to Chimney Rock at the northern boundary of the proposed Wildland Recreation Area. A bed of massive, coarse-grained, light grey sandstone formed 70 million years ago comprises the Whaleback Ridge. This sandstone appears as outcrops along the Whaleback Ridge and forms the cap on Chimney Rock.

The landscape has been molded through the ages by moving ice and running meltwaters. Large limestone rocks were deposited on many ridges by glacial ice which moved over all the area except for the Livingstone Range. In the last glacial advance, a valley glacier flowed along the Oldman River valley through the Livingstone Gap, sending tongues of ice northward along valleys east of the Livingstone Range. The glacier left abundant moraine between Miles and Jacknife coulees. The glaciers gouged U-shaped valleys, leaving moraine along Breeding Valley and drift and drumlins in Bob Creek Valley.

Human History

On glacial till deposited over the Whaleback wilderness grew sedges, herbs and grasses. Wildlife, including buffalo, flourished there, attracting hunting peoples. Humans probably lived in southwestern Alberta as long as 12,000 years ago. Although the Whaleback itself has not been formally examined by archaeologists, the Archaeological Survey of Alberta has recorded 150 prehistoric sites, primarily along the Oldman River and its tributaries where ancient people camped and hunted. The Gap at the Whaleback's southwest boundary is among these sites.

A Hudson's Bay Company surveyor named Peter Fidler explored the area with Peigan Indian guides in 1792. In 1858, Captain Blakiston mapped the area while on assignment from the Palliser Expedition to survey passes over the southern Rocky Mountains for possible railway routes. Looking west from the Oldman River in the vicinity of the southeast corner of the proposed Wildland Recreation Area, Blakiston wrote:

> Looking through the Gap in the near range through which the river passes, I saw a very decided dome-shaped mountain . . . . I named it Gould's Dome [today's Tornado

The golden eagle, soarer of foothill skies and predator of Columbian ground squirrels.

Mountain]. The gap through which I had seen this mountain was in the eastern or near range, of very regular form, extending, with the exception of this gap, for a distance of five and twenty miles without a break. The crest of the range was of so regular a form that no point could be selected as a peak. I therefore gave the whole the name of "Livingston's Range."

Blakiston's buffalo hunting forays from his camp at this location would have taken him into the Whaleback wilderness.

Early explorers of the region reported the river as being named for the mythical being or "old man" who created the earth, rivers, valleys and people. For a number of years the name "old man river" thus applied to three rivers: the North Fork or Northwest Branch, today's Oldman River; the Middle Fork, today's Crowsnest River; and the South Fork of the Old Man, today's Castle River. A large open meadow near the Gap at the southwest corner of the Whaleback Wildland Recreation Area was known by native peoples as the Old Man's Playing Ground. It was a major gathering place for Indian games to take place, but artifacts such as large piles of stones have since been washed away by floodwaters of the Oldman River and Racehorse Creek.

The arrival of whites marked the beginning of the end for the buffalo in the Whaleback and in North America. By 1880, buffalo had been hunted to extinction in Alberta. The introduction of cattle then sparked one of Alberta's most stable economic enterprises. Veterinarian Duncan McEachran, a shareholder in the Cochrane Ranch, one of the first major cattle ranches in Alberta, established the Walrond Ranch with its headquarters just beyond the southeast corner of the proposed Wildland Recreation Area. With the financial backing of Sir John Walrond, he leased some 105 221 hectares of grazing land along the Oldman River, including holdings in the Whaleback. In 1884, the Walrond Ranch purchased more than 3,000 cattle, herding them from Montana to stock their vast grassland holdings.

A tightly managed operation, Walrond Ranch produced fine stock, some of which was exported to England. The Ranch also held a contract with the Indian Department to supply beef to the newly established reserves. When settlers began to arrive in the area, Dr. McEachran held firm to his stand that the semi-arid nature of the land was suitable for ranching, but not farming. Unpopular among the sod busters during the "Walrond War on Settlers", McEachran required police escort for 18 months after being shot at. But McEachran was no match for the new settlers. As newcomers continued to arrive, land prices soared, and around 1946

the Waldron[1] Ranch disposed of all its ranch lands to a Nevada entrepreneur. Today's Waldron Grazing Co-op uses some of the original ranch lands.

Sporadic small-scale coal mining took place in the Whaleback during the period from 1914 to 1932. Three mines operated near the mouth of Bob Creek: the Wilson-Dennis coal mine site (1914-15); the Bob Creek coal mine site (1923-32); and the Jeffrey Coal Mine. Bob Creek apparently bears the name of "Old Man Bob" who had one of the coal mines. Sales were made to the local market created by settlers and ranchers.

The ranch buildings along Bob Creek within the Whaleback are part of the original Gregory "Flying E" ranch headquarters which was later purchased as a branch of the A-7 Ranch. The A-7 ranch itself was started by A.E. Cross, the founder of the Calgary Brewery and one of the famous "Big Four" who started the Calgary Stampede.

Vegetation

The Whaleback landscape is complex and diverse, with geological formations, moisture regimes and soil types that create a kaleidoscope of plant and animal life.

White spruce, Engelmann spruce and

---

[1]   Interestingly, even though the ranch was originally named after Sir John Walrond, it was later known as the Waldron Ranch.

aspen poplar trees carpet broad valley floors in the northern segment of the Whaleback. Willow, dwarf birch, sedges and mosses grow in areas of poor drainage throughout this wilderness, particularly where runoff from springs accumulates. Balsam poplar thrives along the creeks. Small marshes and wet meadows are productive habitats for plants and animals. Blue camas, not commonly found so far north, colours several of these wet depressions with their tall, blue stalks and deep-blue flowers. The root of blue camas was a food staple harvested and stored by native people. The Kootenay also used its nutritious dried bulbs as trading stock. Some today speculate that this plant's distribution in Alberta relates to this Kootenay activity.

Grass covers most valley floors of the southern Whaleback Wildland as well as the warm, dry south- and west-facing slopes of the ridges throughout the area. *Conimitella williamsii*, a herb that is rare in Canada, grows here along with loco-weed, a plant toxic to cattle. White dwarf fleabanes, dwarf larkspur, puccoon, golden bean and yellow balsam root flowers cloak the grasslands of the Whaleback in spring. The white dwarf fleabane is rare in Canada and grows profusely only where conditions are optimum. The balsam root, on the other hand, with its bright sunflower-like bloom, carpets the hills. Uncommon species in the Whaleback include alpine foxtail, kittentails, alum-root, and sweet cicely.

Douglas fir, white and Engelmann spruce and lodgepole pine are the dominant tree species in the proposed Wildland Recreation Area, with isolated groves of limber pine on dry, wind-blown ridges. The Whaleback's Douglas fir stands, with

many trees over 400 years old, are among the oldest and healthiest in the province, and, along with the area's limber pine stands, are believed to be some of the most extensive in Alberta. Unlike the Porcupine Hills, extensive Douglas fir savannahs can be found here. Engelmann spruce dominate the steep east slope of the Livingstone Range. Tundra occurs at higher elevations on this range where the soil is thin and the climate harsh. Idaho and rough fescue, Parry's oat grass, bluebunch wheat grass and shrubby cinquefoil dominate the grassland.

Wildlife

The Whaleback's sunny, grassy slopes are prime wintering range for increasing numbers of elk. Like buffalo, elk were hunted to near extinction during the early days of human settlement in Alberta. The plains buffalo perished but elk persisted, and the herds made a comeback in Alberta during the 1940s and 1950s. An estimated 6,000 elk were believed to have roamed southern Alberta during a population peak in the 1960s. In winter, many foraged on the chinook-blown hills of the Whaleback Wildland. But elk populations declined again where range conditions changed as a result of fire suppression and easy motor vehicle access to their habitat provided by road construction. Climate and the grazing of cattle on former elk winter range were also factors in their decline.

Since the mid-1970s, elk have been increasing chiefly due to mild winters. The Whaleback, along with the proposed Panther

Corners Wildland Recreation Area, is one of the most important elk winter ranges in the province and perhaps in North America. Unlike the winter herds of Panther Corners which spend their summers within the protected confines of Banff National Park, the herds of the Whaleback winter ranges do not spend any time within a park. These herds summer along the Continental Divide, to the west of the Whaleback, including lands within the proposed Upper Oldman Wildland Recreation Area, which has the largest concentration of summering elk. About 1,300 elk winter in the Whaleback area, with some migrating from over 50 kilometres away. The actual migration routes of these elk are still largely unknown. The ability of large herds to disappear from one area and reappear several kilometres away the next day with no more than their tracks to indicate their passing has given elk a magical quality reflected in native mythology and story telling.

The Whaleback hosts many wildlife species, from grassland species like the western meadowlark, sagebrush vole, Richardson's ground squirrel and Nuttall's cottontail to mountain species like the golden-mantled ground squirrel and the dipper.

Cursory field studies in the Whaleback revealed several rare or uncommon species of birds. The golden eagle and prairie falcon nest among rock outcrops, while the upland sandpiper is found in the moist grasslands of this wilderness. The pileated woodpecker, requiring at least several square kilometres per breeding pair, finds suitable mature woodland in the proposed Wildland Recreation Area.

Other birds include Cassin's finch; the blue grouse whose gutteral hooting during spring

FACING PAGE: *The rounded hills of the Whaleback ridge rise like the vertebrae of a humpback whale.* ABOVE: *Trying one's luck for trout in Camp Creek.*

courtship can be heard in older, higher elevation forests; the mountain chickadee; and the solitary vireo, a shy species not found in large numbers anywhere else in the province.

The Whaleback provides prime habitat for a number of mammals whose provincial ranges have been significantly reduced. These include the cougar, grizzly bear, and wolf, all of which prefer large undisturbed territories. Black bears, coyotes, moose, mule deer and Columbian ground squirrels are common in this wilderness. The sagebrush vole and Nuttall's cottontail, which prefer dry, sparse grassland, are found at their most northerly limit in the Whaleback, while the wood frog, a boreal species, is found here at its most southerly limit.

The Whaleback isn't noted for its fisheries, although Camp Creek contains cutthroat trout and Bob Creek contains bull trout. Rocky Mountain whitefish are found in both. These creeks are tributaries to the Oldman River, which is noted for superb trout fishing.

Recreation

From the open, rolling hills along the Whaleback's eastern side to the steep east face of the Livingstone Range on the west, the proposed Wildland Recreation Area provides numerous possibilities for hikes or horseback rides which can be matched to individual abilities and preferences. The open, expansive nature of its forests and grasslands, along with its complex system of ridges, provides a multitude of looped routes.

Trails through these highly scenic wilderness lands meander along valleys, follow old truck trails and cutlines, and traverse steep ridges to hilltops with spectacular views. The Whaleback Ridge itself, an excellent ridge walk or ride, sports a fine view of the sharp, rocky face of the Livingstone Range to the west, the broad valley of the Oldman River in the south, and across the Happy Valley to the Porcupine Hills and the prairie beyond in the east.

The chinook winds, which enable wildlife to winter in this habitat, make snow conditions too unpredictable for most winter sports, although the scarcity of snow and the relatively warm climate permit hiking and horseback riding almost year-round.

Allotting time for exploring the natural history of these wilderness lands is a must for any trip. The most diverse collection of plant communities within the area can be found along Bob Creek and east across the Whaleback Ridge to the ridge of hills which includes Black Mountain on the eastern boundary of the Whaleback Wildland.

Fishing is limited within the proposed Wildland Recreation Area due to the low productivity of the streams. On the other hand, elk and deer hunting is very good. The Whaleback is a primary hunting destination of Calgarians and other southern Albertans.

Access

Access to the Whaleback is provided by Highway 22 running along its eastern boundary, a gravel road running along its south boundary on the north side of the Oldman River to Bob Creek, and the Chimney Rock road entering from the north.

Random vehicle access camping is allowed along the Oldman River road which leads into Bob Creek and also continues further west to Camp Creek. A formal campground, Maycroft, exists at the Highway 22 crossing of the Oldman River.

Land Use Concerns and Recommendations

The Whaleback's wilderness attributes have been harmed somewhat by the completion of a 500 kilovolt powerline which parallels the Whaleback Ridge on the east, extending through Big Coulee Valley. The Alberta Wilderness Association was unsuccessful in convincing the government's regulatory board that a more appropriate route existed further east in Happy Valley where the landscape is already interrupted by Highway 22. Construction of the line was completed through the Whaleback area in 1985.

Grazing

At one time, overgrazing by livestock seriously threatened the supply of forage for elk and deer. The Whaleback is still used extensively for grazing although it is now more carefully controlled by local ranchers and the Alberta government. Concerns today relate to the trampling and siltation of stream banks and springs by cattle. When this occurs at important headwaters, siltation degrades downstream water quality for fish as well as for domestic and recreational users.

The well regulated use of the Whaleback for cattle grazing is compatible with the goals of a Wildland Recreation Area, but a continued balance between cattle, elk and deer still needs to be guaranteed. Range management to reduce trampling of streams and springs should be a primary consideration in the area.

Logging

The Whaleback currently holds little appeal for large-scale logging operations, although small operators once logged and may again log its scattered stands of healthy coniferous trees. Two companies currently have timber quota rights which encompass the Whaleback, but there are no plans to let out timber cutting licences within the near future.

In the winter of 1985, the Alberta Forest Service conducted a major program, removing limber pine infected with mountain pine beetle from the Whaleback ridge. This selective logging was done despite inconclusive evidence that the beetle infecting limber pine, a non-commercial tree, is the same one that attacks the commercially valuable lodgepole pine. This program is regrettable in an area whose primary use is for wilderness recreation and wildlife habitat.

The Alberta Forest Service, which manages most of the proposed Wildland Recreation Area as part of the Bow-Crow Forest Reserve, provides intensive fire protection for the Whaleback. In some areas, dead matter accumulating on the forest floor restricts new growth. While uncontrolled fire is certainly not promoted, a wise management plan for this area should recognize the role of fire in enhancing animal habitat and maintaining the natural vegetation patterns.

Coal, Oil and Gas

Petroleum companies have not shown significant interest in the Whaleback. This could change. Seismic lines from exploration in the 1960s still scar the land and provide unwanted routes for motorized use. Exploration continues near the Whaleback, although no producing wells have been established. In 1985, 23 percent of the Whaleback was under oil and gas lease. It is hoped that these leases can be phased out.

The Whaleback from the top of the Whaleback Ridge eastward falls within Category III of the 1976 Coal Policy. This classification permits coal exploration and development. However, these lands are presently zoned as Critical Wildlife under the Eastern Slopes Policy, which should preclude coal development. Very little interest has been shown for developing coal here since the 1940s.

Motorized Use

At present, cutlines, roads and open terrain provide easy access for vehicles, a factor which is causing considerable damage to wildlife habitat, particularly the grasslands. Access roads inside the proposed Wildland Recreation Area beyond those leading to the ranch buildings on Bob Creek and the camping area at Camp Creek should be reclaimed to discourage vehicle use. Forms of recreation should be encouraged which do not devalue the land for wildlife, domestic grazing, watershed, and non-motorized recreational pursuits.

Ecological Reserve

The Alberta Wilderness Association encourages the establishment of a proposed 25 square kilometre ecological reserve within the area. This candidate ecological reserve representing the montane ecosystem encompasses 12 percent of the proposed Whaleback Wildland Recreation Area. However, the proposed reserve does not encompass enough of the important wildlife range nor a sufficient area for wilderness recreation. Special zoning and legislation is necessary to recognize the Whaleback's recreational and wilderness value, and to ensure its future as a wilderness landscape.

South Castle
A Wilderness for Tomorrow

Like miniature sailboats, the mayfly duns spread across the tail of the pool. Drifting downstream they rode into the rushing currents of the riffle. Here, the mayflies were being funnelled toward a large spruce lodged in the stream.

I saw a trout rise twice in the shelter of the spruce, but the circle of the rise was small. I prepared to move upstream to the pool above, where two fish were actively working the surface. The trout rose again and another mayfly disappeared. But this rise was different than the others. A dorsal fin had appeared below the rings of the rise. My concentration sharpened.

Wading over a Joseph's coat of stream stones, I positioned myself at the downstream end of the fallen spruce. There was no question now, this

was an exceptional cutthroat trout. Every third or fourth mayfly funnelled toward the spruce by stream currents was disappearing. I watched closely to establish the feeding rhythm of the trout. These mayflies were large blue-winged olives, held in the stream flow by a light drizzle. The trout rose in rapid succession taking two mayflies riding the current funnel together. I stripped line off the reel with shaking hands. Then, my excitement turned to dismay.

Swimming toward me along the opposite bank was a mink. Looking in my direction, the mink paused in the shallows. I whistled, but the current's thunder masked the sound. The mink swam by the steadily rising trout. Less than a rod length away, I watched gin-clear currents playing over his back. Totally enthralled, I could see his

nostrils quiver with the scent of this strange object across the stream. Then he glided from view, his tail acting as a rudder as he rounded the bend below. Good fishing, friend.

My gaze caught the trout rising again. The tippet straightened perfectly, dropping the size 12 Adams into the current funnel. A natural mayfly disappeared ahead of the Adams. Was the rhythm right? The Adams passed along the spruce undisturbed.

Cast again, the Adams joined a natural in the current funnel. Both flies arrived in the feeding lane at the same time. A nose appeared, and the natural was gone. I'd been holding my breath – perhaps the next. Then the Adams disappeared. I lifted the rod gently and the line tightened. The trout shook her head as I put

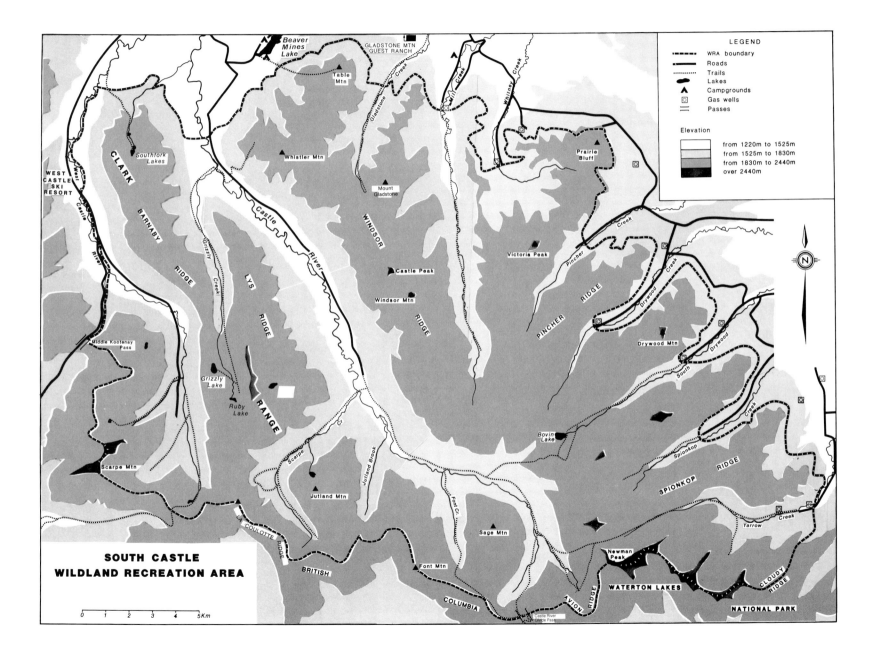

LEGEND

- - - - WRA boundary
——— Roads
········ Trails
⬭ Lakes
▲ Campgrounds
◉ Gas wells
═ Passes

Elevation

	from 1220m to 1525m
	from 1525m to 1830m
	from 1830m to 2440m
	over 2440m

Beaver Mines Lake
GLADSTONE MTN GUEST RANCH
Table Mtn
Gladstone Creek
Whitney Creek
Prairie Bluff
Whistler Mtn
WEST CASTLE SKI RESORT
CLARK
Southfork Lakes
BARNABY
RIDGE
Castle River
Grizzly Creek
West Castle River
WINDSOR
Mount Gladstone
Castle Peak
Windsor Mtn
Victoria Peak
Pincher Creek
PINCHER RIDGE
Drywood Creek
Drywood Mtn
South Drywood
LYS RIDGE
Middle Kootenay Pass
Grizzly Lake
Ruby Lake
RANGE
Scarpe Mtn
Scarpe
Jutland Mtn
Jutland Brook
Cr.
Bovin Lake
Spionkop
SPIONKOP RIDGE
Yarrow Creek
Font Cr.
Sage Mtn
Newman Peak
CLOUDY RIDGE
COULOTTE RIDGE
BRITISH
Font Mtn
AVION RIDGE
WATERTON LAKES
NATIONAL PARK
COLUMBIA
Castle River Divide Pass

SOUTH CASTLE WILDLAND RECREATION AREA

0   1   2   3   4   5Km

more pressure on the rod. Then she exploded in a twisting leap that sent spray onto the shore. Running line from the reel, she crossed the riffle into the pool above.

I beached the trout in the shallows of a point bar. Kneeling on fine gravels, I kept a cushion of water protecting her as the barbless hook fell free. I fumbled in my vest for a tape measure and a camera. That done, I gently held her upright in the currents. My hands ached with the cold. Then she struggled free and was gone. This trout would survive, perhaps to challenge my friend another day.

Large white flowering plumes of bear grass set against the backdrop of sparkling alpine lakes hung among coloured mountain peaks of red, grey, black and buff rock have become a wilderness scene synonymous with the proposed South Castle Wildland Recreation Area.

The Wildland's 474 square kilometres of low mountain peaks, alpine ridges and U-shaped subalpine valleys provides excellent habitat for a variety of Rocky Mountain wildlife. In conjunction with Waterton Lakes National Park on its southern boundary, this area contains a unique array of plants. The majority of Alberta's rarer plants are found here.

The South Castle Wildland is known internationally to hunters for the record-class trophy elk, bighorn ram and cougar which have been taken from the area. Its alpine fishing lakes, excellent Class I fishing streams, ample high country hiking and trail riding routes, and superb

mountain scenery have been enjoyed by many southern Albertans.

White water shoots over falls and plunges into pools through red and orange coloured rock gorges in the canyon country of the eastern or front range segment of this proposed Wildland Recreation Area. Peaks of the Clark Range with lakes set in glacier-carved alpine basins form the western and southern boundaries, encompassing the lake-studded high rock ridges of Barnaby and Lys and the broad flats of the West Castle and South Castle rivers.

About the same size as Waterton Park, the South Castle Wildland shares many of the park's fine qualities, but without its summer crowds. The Wildland provides important bighorn sheep, mountain goat, elk and grizzly bear range. The small size and high elevation of Waterton make protection of the surrounding wild landscapes of the South Castle important to the integrity of this international peace park. In 1979 the international biosphere reserve incorporating Waterton Lakes and Glacier National Park and the surrounding lands within the natural ecosystem, including the South Castle, was established as a sphere of international cooperation and research.

The Wildland's importance as a watershed is indisputable. It is the birthplace of waters for the Castle and Waterton rivers. This region has the highest recorded annual precipitation within the Eastern Slopes.

Unfortunately, unlike most of the proposed Wildland Recreation Areas, the South Castle over the last few decades has experienced the heavy hand of resource development. Much of its mature forest has been logged. Oil and gas

exploration seismic lines scar most of its valleys. Yet, within the area, scenic, wild solitude can still be found. Its recreational, watershed, wildlife and fisheries value and its value to the integrity of Waterton Lakes National Park are too important not to continue to strive to protect its wildlands, and allow rehabilitation to a wilderness area. This generation will not have the pleasure of seeing the valley untouched by the scars of clear-cut logging, but if protection begins today, the next generation will. Providing immense pleasure for today's visitors, the South Castle is indeed "a wilderness for tomorrow".

Geology

Between 60 and 70 million years ago, a major fault in the region, the Lewis Thrust Fault, gave way to massive pressures shoving an enormous block of late Precambrian rock strata eastward over much younger Mesozoic formations. High, jagged mountains of this billion-year-old Precambrian rock were pushed up and over the existing plains. In the South Castle area, the edge of the Lewis Thrust Fault is marked by the abrupt rise of Spreadeagle, Drywood, Prairie Bluff and Table Mountains from the foothills.

The Precambrian strata also contains a 61-metre-thick layer of dark green basalt, a type of volcanic rock that was once laid down on the surface of the earth, then through the millenia subsequently buried under layers of sedimentary rock.

This layer of basalt known as Purcel Lava

extends through the northern U.S. Rockies northward about 50 kilometres into Canada's Waterton Lakes National Park and the proposed South Castle Wildland Recreation Area. This area of southwest Alberta and an area including the Milk River canyon in southeast Alberta are the only locations of exposed volcanic rock in the province. Noticeable because of its colour contrast with lighter sedimentary rock, this hard, dark green rock can be seen exposed on many canyon walls, eroded slopes and cliffs in the South Castle Wildland.

In the exposed Precambrian strata, visitors can see grey, white or green limestones, dolomites and quartzites, and bright red, orange and pink argillites.

Also brought to the surface during mountain building was solidified mud with cracks and ripples from ancient marine environments. Fossils of colonial algae, some of the older fossils of the Rockies, have also been found in the proposed South Castle Wildland Recreation Area.

Some of the mountain peaks in the South Castle are capped with the drab buff-coloured rocks of the younger Paleozoic age. Those rocks range in composition from quartzites to carbonates.

Unlike most of the Eastern Slopes, the extreme southwest of Alberta contains no active glaciers, although past glaciation played an important part in shaping the area's landscape. Glaciers and their meltwater etched the broad, U-shaped valleys, stream terraces and steep canyons of the area. Cirques gouged into mountainsides by glaciers now contain lakes or tarns such as Bovin and Southfork lakes. An impressive example of a cirque is perched atop

a 180 metre cliff at the headwaters of Mill Creek.

In the process of gouging out lower V-shaped valleys into their present U-shape, glaciers cut off the sloping mouths of higher tributary valleys, leaving them as hanging valleys with streams tumbling to the main valley several hundred meters below. An example of such a picturesque valley can be seen in Yarrow Canyon. Glaciers also carved the sharp horns and knife-edged ridges or arêtes at Mount Victoria and Windsor Ridge.

Human History

Prehistoric peoples lived in southwestern Alberta up to 12,000 years ago. At various times over the last 8,000 years, they used a site near Crowsnest Lake northwest of the South Castle as a base for fall and summer hunts into the surrounding wilderness. The Kootenay Indians, once inhabitants of the Waterton Lakes area, often travelled into the proposed Wildland Recreation Area via the Castle River Divide and Middle Kootenay passes. Their stone cairns, up to 300 years old, still mark some of their trails. Plains Indians also hunted and camped in the South Castle wilderness, which was sometimes cause for conflict.

About 280 years ago, the Blackfoot people forced the Kootenays westward from the area and became the last in a series of native cultures to inhabit the region before the arrival of the white man. The loose alliance of the Blackfoot people, which consisted of the Peigan, Blood and

Blackfoot tribes, then inhabited an area from Waterton to the North Saskatchewan River. They often destroyed the foothills camps of the other Indians in order to assert their territorial rights over the bountiful hunting grounds of southwestern Alberta.

During the late 1700s and early 1800s, the Kootenays would slip eastward across the Rocky Mountain passes to hunt bison on the foothills and plains, or to raid Peigan and Blood camps, especially in the vicinity of Crowsnest Pass. Out of fear that the Kootenays would obtain firearms from white traders, the plains Indians closed the passes of the southern Rockies for about the first 70 years of the last century.

Under the guidance of Kootenay Indians, two voyageurs appointed by David Thompson, La Bossi and Le Blare, crossed a southern pass believed to be the Middle Kootenay Pass in the late 1700s. Lieutenant Blakiston of the Palliser Expedition was the first white person to record the South Castle area. From a vantage point about 50 kilometres north, he named Castle Mountain for "the resemblance to a castle on its summit." Although guides in 1792 told Hudson's Bay Company surveyor Peter Fidler of the existence of Crowsnest Pass while he was in the Livingstone Gap area, Blakiston was not informed of the Pass. In 1857, he instead crossed the North Kootenay Pass which lies north of the South Castle area and south of the Crowsnest.

While the Blackfoot were "newcomers" 280 years ago, it wasn't until the turn of the century that white newcomers actually populated the region. Lush valley bottoms in the southern portion of the proposed Wildland Recreation Area were ideal for cattle grazing and were in use by the turn of the century. Settlers often hauled logs from the valleys to build homes and barns. With the start of railway construction through Crowsnest Pass in 1897, large operators moved into the region to log.

By 1914, cart trails existed along the old horse trails up the West Castle and South Castle valleys. In that same year, Waterton Lakes National Park, which had been established in 1895, was enlarged to encompass today's entire proposed Wildland Recreation Area, as well as all lands north to the Carbondale River. Later in 1921, the 1295-square-kilometre national park was drastically cut back to near its present size of 526 square kilometres. The South Castle wilderness, now outside the protective boundaries of the national park, reverted to the Crowsnest National Forest and was maintained as a provincial game preserve until 1954. In the game preserve all types of predators were trapped and shot, and extensive grazing by cattle, horses and sheep was permitted.

In 1934, a major fire burned from Whistler Mountain south to what was then called Meadow Cache. Meadow Cache, a food cache for patrolling forest rangers, was located in the head of the South Castle at the foot of Sage Mountain. On the heels of this fire, in 1936 an even larger fire swept over the Middle Kootenay Pass area from the Flathead region in British Columbia and burned north and east. The 250 men at the Lynx Creek Forestry station, equipped with just horses and hand tools, could do little to stop it. The fire burned itself out in late September of that year. The 20-foot-wide wagon trail the Forest Service had earlier cleared to the head of the South Castle was later covered by deadfall.

Elk, rarely seen in the area prior to the 1930s, flourished on the expanse of new grass in the wake of the fires. By the late 1940s, the elk were estimated to number 3,000 in the region. Extensive domestic grazing and the over-population of elk took a heavy toll on the range lands. Owing to competition for forage between game and domestic stock, the government in 1950 decided to gradually eliminate horse and sheep grazing from the area and to cut back on the number of cattle by over one-half. The last sheep grazing permit, which was on Yarrow Creek, was discontinued in 1954, and horse permits were discontinued in 1956. The game preserve was eliminated and hunting opened in 1954. Six hundred elk were apparently killed the first day of the season.

Vegetation

Climate, topography and past glacial history in the southwest corner of Alberta allow a unique combination of vegetation to flourish. Over one hundred species of plants have been identified in the proposed Wildland Recreation Area that occur nowhere else in Alberta. Because it lies in the path of a major storm track from the Pacific Ocean, this southwest corner of Alberta enjoys warmer temperatures and greater precipitation than the remainder of the Eastern Slopes to the north. The terrain in the Wildland Recreation Area ranges from plains to high mountain peaks, prompting an unusual mixing of prairie and alpine vegetation in some places.

Another reason for the unique vegetation is the existence of areas which remained unglaciated during the last ice age. Plants living in the unglaciated areas subsequently spread through the southwest.

Since the early 1970s, clearcut logging throughout the proposed Wildland Recreation Area has significantly altered the natural vegetation and scenery of the area. A spruce bark beetle outbreak triggered extensive logging of the native spruce in the upper reaches of the West Castle during the 1970s. During the 1980s, clearcut logging directed at salvaging timber killed by the mountain pine beetle was conducted on Gladstone Creek, Table Mountain and along the upper reaches of the South Castle, including Front Creek, the west side of Windsor Ridge and around the lake at the top of Sheep Creek in the very head of the South Castle. In the early 1900s, selective logging and small patch clearcuts were done in Mill Creek.

Although the South Castle has a maritime-type climate, chinook winds from the southwest frequently dry the landscape. The vegetation type on each slope is determined by the direction each slope faces and each slope's elevation. Grasses, stunted limber pine, mats of bearberry, juniper and big sagebrush can be found on the slopes exposed to the chinook winds. In contrast, the sheltered and moister north- and east-facing slopes are carpeted with forests of aspen poplar, Douglas fir, white spruce, Engelmann spruce and alpine fir.

The terrain and scenery along the east side of Windsor and Victoria ridges in the eastern portion is quite different from the remaining western portion of the proposed Wildland Recreation Area. From mountains rising abruptly above the foothills, turbulent streams flow eastward and northward through deep, steep-sided canyons and gorges. In this area, thickets of willow, aspen poplar and balsam poplar line the creek banks.

On the valley sides, there are open meadows on south-facing slopes and alpine fir broken by avalanche tracks on north-facing slopes. Or, in the case of Mill, Gladstone and Whitney Creek valleys, the lower reaches are forested with lodgepole pine, and the very upper reaches contain mature white and Engelmann spruce along with alpine fir occurring still higher up. Because of ever-present winds and the winter chinooks in the canyons, the higher elevation alpine fir forests are stunted, wind-pruned and red tinged.

The terrain further west is characterized by the broad, U-shaped valleys of the South and West Castle rivers flanked by wide gravel bars and dramatic mountain peaks. The middle and lower sections of these main valleys and the lower reaches of their tributaries show various stages of regrowth, after having been swept by fire in the 1930s. Lodgepole pine, a fire successional tree, is the dominant species in these areas. The remainder of the valley floors are a mixture of lodgepole pine, aspen poplar and white spruce. Here the understory of the spruce/pine forests includes false huckleberry and white-flowered rhododendrons. In the deep shade of the coniferous forests the rare one-flowered Clintonia can be found, and in rather damp areas of the woods the uncommon foam flower is often sheltered.

Douglas fir can be found in small stands on dry valley walls. Small pockets of alpine fir and Engelmann spruce occur on some higher valley slopes and in the valley headwaters, indicating areas which have escaped the recent fires. Forest growth is especially lush in the valley headwaters

where the soils are deep and moist.

Within the proposed Wildland Recreation Area, sites along the West Castle valley have a number of rare or uncommon plant species. Here, the western red cedar, a common British Columbia tree, can be found along with extensive stands of white-bark pine on the steep southeast-facing slopes. White-bark pine 25 metres high provide an open canopy for a number of uncommon Alberta plants including mountain lover, thimbleberry and bear grass. A member of the lily family, bear grass, with its impressive plume of small white flowers, has become synonymous with the southwest. Its leaves were used by Indians for basket weaving, and it is also eaten by bears in spring.

A rare vegetation community occurs on the north and west sides of Whistler Mountain. Volcanic soil and rock debris at this site encourage the growth of plants similar to those found in the big sagebrush vegetation of dry areas in eastern Oregon, Washington and southern British Columbia. This unusual collection includes rice grass, deer brush, mountain maple, creeping grape, mariposa lily, perennial lupine, and Alaska bog orchid.

On the mountain sides below approximately 1830 metres elevation are forests of alpine fir and scattered white-bark pine. The rare yellow monkey-flower is a plant of wet mossy places found at middle to low elevations. It can be easily identified by its bright, crimson-speckled flowers. The subalpine forests disappear at treeline with only the hardiest white-bark pine and alpine fir surviving. Alpine larch, with its deciduous needles that turn brilliant orange in fall, grows on sheltered slopes at treeline. Usually only seen as scattered clumps in the Rockies, extensive

stands of these trees grow on Barnaby Ridge and Sage Mountain.

Alpine areas have the typical plants as well as the rarer southwest plants, including Lyall's beard-tongue and stonecrop on the south-facing exposed rocky areas. The large lavender flowers of Lyall's beard-tongue adorn the high, rocky areas.

In moist habitats, other rare plants can be found, such as white angelica, yellow angelica and Geyer's onion.

It is certainly no exaggeration to say that the majority of Alberta's rare plants can be found in this region. Those interested in viewing these plants are well advised to take along a copy of Job Kuijt's *Flora of Waterton Lakes National Park*.

Wildlife

Besides encouraging unique and diverse plant growth, the terrain and climate of the proposed Wildland Recreation Area provide excellent habitat for mountain goats, Rocky Mountain bighorn sheep, mule and whitetailed deer, elk, moose, cougar and grizzly bear. Warm chinook winds expose grasslands on the southwest faces of the numerous ridges and valleys during winter, providing forage for wildlife. The eastern or front range portion of the South Castle Wildland, extending eastward from Whistler Mountain and Windsor Ridge, includes some of the most productive bighorn sheep range in North America.

Large herds of bighorns once roamed the

canyons of Yarrow, Spionkop, Drywood, South Drywood and Pincher creeks, wintering on the southwest-facing slopes of Barnaby and Windsor ridges and Table and Whistler mountains. Development of the Waterton Gas Field with well roads leading up each valley has suppressed their numbers. Unfortunately, these bighorn herds recently fell victim to a major outbreak of bacterial pneumonia which also attacked southern British Columbia herds. During 1982-83, 40 to 60 percent of this South Castle population died.

In addition to providing bighorn sheep habitat, the cliff walls of Barnaby Ridge are good mountain goat habitat. Bands of mountain goats can also be seen in the peaks of the Clark Range at Font, Jutland and Scarp mountains.

About 600 elk reportedly winter in the entire Castle River region. Most of these spend summer and fall in South Castle Wildland and then move to traditional winter ranges in the low hills on the northern and eastern edges of the Wildland Recreation Area. Unfortunately, domestic livestock compete for grazing land critical to wildlife. Since the introduction of regulated cattle grazing allotments, however, wildlife has made a comeback in South Castle Wildland over the past two decades.

Moose are often seen in the aspen and willow thickets along South Castle and West Castle rivers, and along wooded creek valleys between Mill and Yarrow creeks. Good populations of lynx, cougar, coyote and beaver also inhabit the proposed Wildland Recreation Area. The isolated alpine basins and ample food sources provide superior grizzly habitat, and there are signs that the past closure on grizzly hunting in this part of the province has helped these magnificent creatures regain their foothold in the area. Their smaller cousins, the black bears, also thrive on the lush vegetation, including the prolific huckleberry crops.

Because of the small size of Waterton Lakes National Park and the fact that wildlife populations do not keep to man-made boundaries, all boundary areas between Waterton Park and the proposed Wildland Recreation Area are important for bighorn sheep, mountain goat, elk and grizzly bear.

A full array of mountain and foothill birds can be found in this area, from song birds to upland game birds and birds of prey. Examples include the dark eyed junco, dusky flycatcher, chipping sparrow, mountain bluebird, pine siskin, western tanager, Townsend's and MacGillivary's warblers, fox sparrow, Swainson's thrush and varied thrush, blue grouse, white tailed ptarmigan and the golden eagle.

The South Castle River together with its tributaries is rated as a Class I or excellent natural fishery. The West Castle and its tributaries are rated only slightly less highly. The headwaters of many of the streams are important as brood rearing areas for bull trout and Rocky Mountain whitefish. Spawning and over-wintering areas for fish are found throughout. Good habitat is provided for naturally perpetuating populations of Rocky Mountain whitefish, bull trout and rainbow, cutthroat and eastern brook trout. About half of the 17 alpine lakes in the area also have native sport fish, though their cold waters are not very productive. To meet the sport fishing demand, the lakes are periodically stocked. Golden trout, a native of the California Sierra Mountains, were introduced into three alpine lakes (South Fork, Rainy Ridge and Scarp) in the South Castle Wildland in 1954. Brown trout have been introduced into South Fork Lakes.

Recreation

The South Castle's rugged beauty and accessibility combined with its varied opportunities for hunting, fishing, hiking and horseback riding make these wilderness lands a popular destination, particularly among residents of southern Alberta. Its wild and attractive scenery provides a wilderness backdrop for developed recreation areas adjacent to it: West Castle ski resort, Beauvais Lake Provincial Park, Beaver Mines Lake, and a major guest ranch. Waterton Lakes National Park and British Columbia's Flathead Valley lie along its borders, presenting opportunities for extended wilderness excursions of four or more days.

For the wilderness traveller, the spectacular mountain scenery, the lakes tucked below colourful cliffs, the canyons with water trickling over bright rock, and the abundant animal life of the proposed Wildland Recreation Area delight the senses. Although the South Castle's landscapes have felt the heavy hand of man, much unspoiled beauty remains, the proposed Wildland Recreation Area offers wilderness, including hunting opportunities, which Waterton Park cannot. As well, the traveller still has the opportunity to choose his own itinerary and camp location, a freedom which can no longer be offered in Waterton due to the overcrowding of its limited wilderness lands. Formal protection of the wilderness landscapes of the South Castle and the quality non-motorized recreation these lands offer would relieve the visitor pressures on Waterton Lakes National Park. Neighboring communities and adjacent recreation developments would have the added bonus of increased recreation and tourism revenue.

Hiking and Trail Riding

This corner of Alberta is noted for its strong, westerly winds, sudden spring snowstorms, mild winters and sunny summers. For the prepared visitor, hiking and trail riding in the South Castle are pleasurable experiences which can begin once the snows have melted from high country passes. Earlier trips are best confined to the main valley bottoms and the eastern canyon country. The mountains in the proposed Wildland Recreation Area, the highest just over 2600 metres, are relatively low and gently sloped on at least one side. It is, therefore, possible to hike or ride most mountain crests.

Each of the eight valleys of the canyon country in the eastern front range segment of the proposed Wildland Recreation Area has its own character and special attraction. The area is ideal for day trips, with the possibility of looped routes from one valley to the next. Longer trips can be made into the core of the South Castle, with these routes including a pack trail from Yarrow Creek, a high pass on the north side of Castle Mountain from Mill Creek and a low saddle at the head of South Drywood Creek. A

high country adventure can be taken travelling from the Pincher Creek valley along ridges south to Newman Peak and then along a steep descent too difficult for horses to Goat Lake in Waterton Lakes National Park.

To the west lies the colourful rock of Windsor Ridge, with the rugged turrets of Castle Mountain on its north end, the broad flats of the South Castle River Valley, the 12.5 kilometre Barnaby Ridge with its 300 to 600 metre cliffs, the braided river valley of the West Castle, and finally the Clark Range of peaks which sweeps around the western and southern boundaries of the Wildland Recreation Area with its lake-studded alpine cirques. Pack trails and in some cases seismic lines lead up the side valleys, along ridges and through the passes, with routes also along the top of the Continental Divide and on the ridge line forming the Waterton Park boundary with the South Castle. These latter routes provide exceptional views, as does a hike along Lys Ridge. Font Creek has a lot of scenery packed into its short length, with its waters in the lower section tumbling over falls through a deep gorge of red rock. The lush meadows of Grizzly Creek lead to two deep lakes set below the loose red scree and outcrops of Lys Ridge.

Castle River Divide Pass at the head of the South Castle is a main connecting link for the trail system of Waterton Park and the proposed Wildland Recreation Area. Connoisseurs of wild berries will want to check out the lush huckleberry patches of the Middle Kootenay Pass area and the West Castle Valley.

Due to the small size of Waterton Lakes National Park and of the proposed Wildland Recreation Area, the two commercial outfitters

in the region use these two areas as a contiguous unit for wilderness trips. Day-trips into the proposed Wildland Recreation Area are also outfitted from the adjacent guest ranch.

Winter Sports

The chinook winds in this region which result in mild temperatures also lead to uncertain snow conditions. However, when conditions permit, South Castle, West Castle and Mill Creek valleys are good skiing routes. The main valleys of the South Castle and West Castle are also used by snowmobilers.

Hunting and Fishing

The South Castle's potential for game hunting is believed to have been utilized as long as 10,000 years ago by prehistoric people who hunted deer, elk, bighorn sheep and bison in its elongated mountain valleys.

The area is still popular among hunters and has produced trophy bighorn sheep, elk, cougar and grizzly. The current world's record trophy bighorn ram was taken from this area. The area is home to some 1,500 head of big game, and, if habitat is properly protected, opportunities for quality hunting in the future should be assured.

The South Castle and tributaries constitute some of the best stream fisheries in Alberta, particularly for native cutthroat trout, Rocky Mountain whitefish and bull trout.

Because the streams are such excellent natural fisheries, they are not stocked. However, fish plants have been periodically conducted in

FACING PAGE: *A rare plant in Alberta, bear grass is only found in the southwest corner of the province.* ABOVE: *View down the South Castle from Avion Ridge.*

suitable high altitude lakes. Grizzly Lake, South Fork Lakes, Rainy Ridge Lakes, Bovin Lake, Jutland Lake, Lys Lake and Scarp Lakes all have trout for the adventurous angler.

Land Use Concerns and Recommendations

The proposed South Castle Wildland Recreation Area is a significant portion of the internationally recognized Biosphere Reserve which has the Waterton/Glacier International Peace Park as its core. In 1974, the Alberta government recognized the South and West Castle watershed as having a "very high potential for wildland recreation." Accordingly, the 1977 Eastern Slopes Policy zoned the entire southern portion of the Forest Reserve, including the proposed Wildland Recreation Area, as Prime Protection and General Recreation lands.

Later in 1979, government resource managers concluded that the General Recreation Zone in this area did not provide appropriate protection for the sensitive U-shaped valleys of the subalpine areas or for the integrity of the north boundary of Waterton Lakes National Park. Therefore, planners proposed that almost the entire South Castle Wildland Recreation Area be zoned as Prime Protection, leaving only the northern valley segment of the South Castle as General Recreation Zone lands.

This, however, was reversed in 1985. Only the alpine vegetation zone and Grizzly, Scarp and Jutland creeks are now zoned as Prime Protection, leaving Font Creek and the headwaters of South Castle up to the alpine vegetation zone open to controlled development including proposed gas exploration and development. Gladstone, Mill and Whitney Creek drainages below the alpine are now Multiple Use lands allowing for the full spectre of resource development.

Logging

In 1973, government assessors reported that problems had been experienced in the Castle River region in satisfying holders of timber quotas. "In some areas the headwaters of streams have been allowed to be logged, including some protection forest, in order to meet the quotas." This situation changed little in the following years. A spruce beetle epidemic which took hold of blown-down timber in 1970 triggered extensive logging in the headwaters of the West Castle River. Then in the 1980s, a mountain pine beetle infestation broke out in the mature lodgepole pine stands, precipitating a new round of salvage logging. Scarp Creek, with a small area of around 100 hectares slated for salvage logging, was in the end left untouched.

Today, the future of the few remaining stands of mature forest in the proposed Wildland Recreation Area is uncertain. All lands with the exception of the alpine zone and the rugged high elevation valleys of Scarp, Grizzly and Jutland creeks are included in the permanent timber land base to be managed for future timber production and logging. Sanitation logging, which is done to inhibit the spread of disease or insect damage, would be permitted in the Scarp, Grizzly and Jutland drainages.

Oil and Gas

One of Alberta's early gas wells was located in the Middle Kootenay Pass area on the northwest boundary of the proposed Wildland Recreation Area. Immediately adjacent to the east boundary of the area is the Waterton Gas Field, which was discovered in 1957. With its 32 flowing or capped wells and two gas injection wells, service road infrastructure, and gas processing plant, this major resource development has seriously undermined the wildlife and recreation potential of the front range on the edge of the proposed Wildland Recreation Area. With the priority being to develop this gas field to its fullest potential, it is possible that further exploration and drilling could extend westward into the proposed Wildland Recreation Area. However, the gas field has a projected lifespan to the year 2000, after which it is hoped that reclamation will begin.

The discovery of the Waterton Gas Field stimulated further seismic exploration throughout the South Castle Wildland. Oil and gas leases cover a significant portion of the area. The provincial government's land use zoning and management of the area would permit exploration drilling and development into the very headwaters of the South Castle adjacent to the Waterton Park boundary.

Motorized Use

As is the case throughout almost all of the Eastern Slopes, the roads and seismic lines associated with past resource activities now dictate present recreational use.

The South Castle Wildland is bisected by old resource roads up the West and South Castle valleys, along with seismic lines up most creek valleys in the area. As of 1985, motorized use is still permitted throughout the entire area. In 1982, the 13 kilometre headwater section of the South Castle road was reclaimed by the Alberta Forest Service, but motor vehicle use had laid that work to waste by the fall of 1982, and it remains a popular route for vehicles. Due to the topography, recontouring work done on 10 kilometres of the Grizzly seismic line and five kilometres of the abandoned road up Scarp Creek has been more successful in controlling some of the motorized use within the proposed Wildland Recreation Area.

Recently, there appears to be an increase in vehicular use in the proposed Wildland Recreation Area, particularly along seismic lines. In order to protect the wildlife, fisheries and wilderness recreation potentials, the South Castle area's network of seismic lines and other access routes should be reclaimed and legally closed to motorized use.

Coal and Minerals

Exploration permits issued for the Spionkop Ridge area in 1963 and 1964 resulted in a find of ore containing copper, silver and uranium. Because the area involved is composed of steep alpine slopes and provides critical winter range for bighorn sheep, in 1985 the provincial government allowed these lands to remain in the Prime Protection Zone and off-limits for mining.

There is no coal of commercial interest within the proposed South Castle Wildland Recreation Area.

Grazing

There are three grazing allotments in the South Castle Wildland, the largest being in the South Castle River drainage basin. All are rated in fair and stable condition, though many years of wildfire suppression has resulted in a gradual loss of grassland for cattle and wildlife. Domestic grazing is primarily concentrated in the valley bottoms. In the past, domestic livestock have overgrazed many areas, threatening food resources for wildlife. Stabilization is now occurring. The number of cattle permitted to graze on allotments has decreased in the past 10 years, and if key wildlife range and the watershed are protected from damage by cattle, grazing could remain a compatible use. However, in 1985, the government proposed clearing of new range and an increase in domestic grazing.

Ecological Reserves

Three sites were under consideration as potential Ecological Reserves: along Grizzly Creek, in the headwaters of the West Castle and along the South Castle. The 259 hectare South Castle site encompassing the rare big sagebrush plant community remains as a candidate Ecological Reserve.

Appendix I

Enjoying the Wilderness

There are many who enjoy our wilderness lands through books, films and art, or as the backdrop to a road or accommodation. However, increasing numbers of people choose to enjoy and experience its wonders first-hand.

Wilderness recreation is one of the least expensive forms of leisure available, and is enjoyed by people of all ages and all walks of life. Everyone can enjoy the wilderness. If you have a disability, there are a number of guides and outfitters in Alberta who will help you with your trip. You can make a wilderness trip as leisurely or as challenging as you want. There are also special facilities within our Eastern Slopes national and provincial parks, as well as service groups who conduct backcountry trips.

If wilderness travel is a new experience for you, there are numerous free pamphlets to help you, and there is probably an AWA chapter, outdoor recreation club or horse group near you which would welcome new or novice participation. Some useful pamphlets available from the AWA as well as government offices are:

- Wilderness Travel in the Eastern Slopes (AWA)

- Backcountry Users Guide (Parks Canada)

- The "Wilderness Safety" series (Alta. Recreation and Parks)

- Guide for Using Horses in Mountain Country (by Robert W. Miller; available from the AWA for $1.00)

- Minimize Your Impact While Hiking and Canoeing (Alta. Recreation and Parks)

- Wildlife and You (Alta. Fish and Wildlife)

- You Are in Bear Country (Parks Canada)

- Four Lines of Defense Against Hypothermia

- The "Enjoy Winter Safely" series (Alta. Recreation and Parks)

- Topographical Maps (Geological Survey of Canada Offices)

Some Things to Remember for Wilderness Travel in the Eastern Slopes

The Basics

- Trails tend to be of a minimal or primitive standard, with some travellable areas lacking any man-made trails. Always carry a compass and the appropriate topographic maps for the area, and know how to use them. A listing of topographic maps for each of the Wildland Recreation Areas is included on page 119 of this book.

- Pre-trip preparation of food, clothing, first-aid equipment and maps for the route to be travelled is essential. So too is a check on the serviceability of all your equipment.

- Mountain and foothill travel is more strenuous than a walk in urban parks or prairie and parkland areas. Allot yourself enough travel time and make sure you have sturdy, comfortable footwear. If you or your horse are new to wilderness recreation, begin exploring short trails first and work up to longer trips.

- Travelling alone is not recommended.

- Many of the higher trails and routes traverse rocky mountain slopes. Most of this terrain is over sedimentary rock which is often loose and unstable. Exercise care when traversing the loose scree slopes, cliffs and boulder fields.

- Familiarize yourself with safe methods of crossing cold, fast-moving streams. Pick broad or braided and slow-moving crossings and move with the current.

- Show good etiquette, no matter if the others you meet are on foot or horse, snowshoe or ski. Those on foot or bicycle should step off the trail to allow horse parties to pass.

- Carry cooking stoves or build only small fires, well guarded by rocks. Put fires out thoroughly with water. Remove all evidence of your fire and bury or scatter the cold ashes.

- Do not litter. Pack out what you pack in.

Weather

The ardent wilderness traveller usually has one eye on the scenery and one on the weather. Weather in the Eastern Slopes is unpredictable. Snow, sleet and freezing rain occur with little warning in the mountains, even on the hottest summer days. At lower elevations, this may only be a minor annoyance or even a refreshing treat, but higher up, these conditions may become a serious problem if hikers or riders are not prepared. Within the Wildland Recreation Areas, there are many trails or routes which are above treeline and thus offer little or no protection from bad weather. Lightning, a common phenomenon in mountain storms, is a serious danger to exposed riders or hikers, especially if they are carrying metal-framed packs.

Lowland summer weather may persuade you to start hiking in shorts, but temperatures drop about one degree every 200 metres in elevation gain, and insects, brush, sudden weather changes and rocks may later prove that long pants are more practical and comfortable. A windbreaker, rain gear (including pants), wool toque, gloves and an extra sweater are standard gear for any trip, even in summer.

Low cloud, fog or snow "white-outs" which can easily obscure landmarks may occur through the year, so be prepared with maps and compass, and turn back if necessary.

Water

For many, drinking from cold, clear mountain streams is a pleasurable part of the wilderness experience. Sadly, a parasitic micro-organism, Giardia lamblia, has been introduced by humans into the waters of the U.S. Rocky Mountains, and has recently caused illnesses in Banff National Park. If ingested by drinking contaminated water, this parasite can cause serious problems such as diarrhea, nausea and severe stomach cramps. These effects can be debilitating, especially in the wilderness. The contamination of wilderness waters with these parasites is due solely to lazy people who don't take the time to bury their body wastes a safe distance (60 metres) from a water course. Other mammals, such as dogs and beavers, can become infected by the contaminated waters and further spread the parasite.

Boiling water thoroughly before using it will usually kill the parasite. However, it won't undo the damage done to once-clean running wilderness waters, so be sure all in your party practise proper backcountry sanitation.

Drinking from seeps and springs where you can see the water's source is considered a safe practice.

Wildlife

Conflicts between wilderness travellers and wildlife that result in injury to humans are very rare. However, a wild animal can be dangerous if not treated with respect. Help ensure that wildlife will continue to thrive in their natural surroundings, so you and your children may continue to enjoy seeing them in our wilderness lands:

- enjoy from a distance

- do not handle or disturb young wildlife

- do not feed wildlife . . . ever

- exercise common sense and reasonable caution

- do not harass wildlife, even to take a picture . . . many animals are much more sensitive than you might believe

- respect wildlife and their home . . . leave nothing behind but your footprints

- know and follow all applicable hunting and fishing regulations.

The probability of a dangerous encounter with a bear is very low, less than that of being struck by lightning and far less than that of being injured while driving to the wilderness area. However, precautions are necessary if this risk is to be kept to a minimum. Precautions focus around the two main themes of food and awareness:

- Control food and garbage. For the sake of those who come after you, leave absolutely no food or garbage behind. While camped, hang food well out of the reach of bears (at least five metres off the ground and away from tree limbs). Carry long fine cord, gloves and a sturdy cloth food bag for rigging food well out of reach.

- Be alert. If possible, warn bears of your presence by making noises, such as shouting, especially in areas where visibility is restricted (as in dense willow) or when you have seen signs of bears. Remember, dense bush and rushing water muffle the sound of noisemakers such as bells.

- Be cautious travelling through, or avoid altogether, areas where bears tend to feed, such as loose soil areas with hedysarum plants, areas of lush vegetation such as horsetail, berry patches and heavily vegetated avalanche slopes.

- Commercially developed pen-sized "bear crackers" (like a flare) are often carried to frighten off bears in an emergency. Boat horns that operate on compressed air to produce a loud sound are also a recommended precautionary device.

- Except for an instance of a rabid wolf biting a man, there is no authenticated instance of North American wolves harming humans. Wolves are very shy.

- Ground squirrels, marmots, pikas and porcupines all enjoy chewing leather and salty camping equipment, as well as soap, food, or even aluminum cookwear on occasion. Take precautions. Don't leave your boots unattended.

Hypothermia

One of the most serious threats to wilderness travellers, yet one which is easily avoided through proper preparation and common sense, is hypothermia. A cooling of the body's core temperature, hypothermia can lead to rapid physical and mental dysfunctions, even death. Contributing factors are cold, wetness, wind chill, fatigue and lack of high energy food. Initial symptoms include persistent shivering, slow, slurred speech, and loss of coordination, especially in the hands. Memory lapse, incoherence and impaired judgement may also occur. The victims may not be aware they are in danger, so their survival depends on someone else. When detected, act immediately to warm the victims and get them into shelter. If possible, place them in a bathtub of warm water. If that is impossible, exchange wet clothing for dry, and get them into a sleeping bag with another person to warm them (skin to skin contact is the most effective; they cannot warm up unaided). Giving the victims warm, sweet drinks will help to revive them.

Environmental Protection

Trails which are often game trails, but are usable by foot, horse, snowshoe or ski provide access within the Wildland Recreation Areas. During your explorations of these wilderness lands, remember, as tough and hardy as those lands may seem, they are actually delicate environments. Many of the proposed Wildland Recreation Areas also contain candidate Ecological Reserves, specific areas recognized by scientists as being unique or representative of our natural heritage. Please make a point of being respectful and considerate of the environment you are enjoying. Many of the lichens, mosses and dwarfed trees of the high exposed areas may be hundreds of years old and can easily be damaged permanently. Learn to minimize the impact of your presence on these special places.

Camping

Choosing a good campsite is a matter of finding a spot that satisfies a number of basic requirements. Unless you are prepared with campstoves and wind-designed tents, and are willing to be extra cautious of the delicate terrain, you should avoid camping in alpine areas. A good campsite should:

- be close to water (but not immediately next to it)

- have flat areas for tents

- be well off trails - to avoid both wildlife and other parties using the trails

- have plenty of feed for horses, if travelling on horse

- have a view - both to provide a warning of wildlife in the area, and for your own pleasure

- have fuel in the form of dry dead wood, if you are planning to use a fire

- have good rocks close by for a fireplace

- be close to tall trees from which to rig your foodbag away from wildlife

- be sheltered from the wind by rocks or trees

- be in a dry area, well out of runoff or flood channels.

The Fire

A commercially available lightweight tubular steel grill about 40 centimetres long allows four to five people to cook comfortably over a very small fireplace. Two elongated flat stones to balance the grill across and a single flat, heat-reflecting stone at one end makes a simple, safe, small and effective fireplace. Remove the duff and some of the topsoil from between the long side stones to deepen the fire box area. Scrape the duff away from the open end of the fireplace. This soil may later be placed back over the wet cold ashes of the extinguished fire to eliminate evidence of your fire. Scatter the rocks too.

Basic Equipment for Hiking Trips

- Waterproof, lightweight tent with mosquito netting.

- Warm clothing, extra woolen socks, rain gear with pants, toque, mitts, sun-shielding hat, sturdy boots with lug soles, long underwear for late summer and fall.

- Warm, lightweight sleeping bag - good to 0°C in summer.

- Mattress for warmth and comfort - "Thermarests" are excellent.

- First-aid kit with such items as wide adhesive tape, band aids, aspirin for headache, anti-histamine pills for bee stings or pollens, suncream, lip cream and ointment for scrapes, cuts and insect bites. The adhesive tape or mole skin can be applied directly to areas of the feet that feel like they are going to blister; if they have already blistered, apply directly and remove at night to allow the blistered area to dry.

- Lightweight, nutritious food, and extra-high-energy items for emergencies.

- Personal kit including soap, face cloth, small towel, toothbrush and paste, small mirror and hair brush, lots of moisturizing cream such as Nivea, and lip cream.

- Nesting cooking pots in a sturdy bag, sturdy non-melting cups, pocket knife, tubular steel grill, scrubbing pad, small container of soap, simple metal utensils.

- Compass and topographic maps in waterproof case.

- Whistle.

- Bear crackers or boat horn.

- Wooden matches in waterproof containers (scatter several of these throughout your gear for added protection against dampness) and a fire starter.

- Mosquito repellent.

- Folding saw (much more lightweight and useful than an axe for tough subalpine wood).

- Camp stove and fuel (if you are not planning on open fires).

- Lightweight water bag.

- Light woolen socks (for most people these are the best to wear next to the skin to prevent blistering and to diffuse moisture).

- Long cord and heavy cloth food bag with plastic cover (a garbage bag is fine) for rigging food away from bears and other animals. Wear gloves to protect the hands while raising food bag or climbing trees.

Appendix II

The AWA – Who We Are

The AWA is the largest citizen group in western Canada working to protect wildlands. We are a non-profit, charitable organization, with a full-time office in Calgary and chapters throughout the province. Tax-deductible donations, grants, bequests and membership dues support our work.

What Do We Do?

- We promote sound ideas for conserving wilderness.

- We work with government, industry, individuals and organizations to encourage careful management of our natural lands and wild rivers.

- We carry out research on Alberta's wildlands and wildland issues.

- We publish books and other literature on wilderness topics.

- We represent our members at public hearings and planning sessions involving wilderness issues.

- We operate resource centres and provide reference materials that anyone can use and learn from.

- We sponsor workshops and conferences on wilderness concerns.

Two Decades of Progress

Formed in 1965 by ranchers, outfitters and backcountry enthusiasts, the Alberta Wilderness Association has become one of the more active environmental groups in the province. We were constituted in 1968.

Among our accomplishments, we successfully promoted Alberta's Wilderness Areas Act of 1971. Because of the restrictive nature of the act, however, we have proposed no additions to the three areas it covers. Instead, the AWA has advocated a series of Wildland Recreation Areas that would allow legislative protection from motorized and industrial activity, but would allow traditional uses such as hunting and fishing and traditional modes of travel like hiking and horseback riding. Apart from proposals along the Eastern Slopes, we are seeking to protect the Rumsey area as the best of the province's remaining aspen parkland, to gain recognition of the unique Milk River and Suffield grasslands, and to set aside the western Swan Hills as an outstanding boreal-forest area and grizzly bear habitat. Many of our ideas are now reflected in Alberta's land-use policies.

Having participated in the development of the province's Eastern Slopes zoning system, we went on to help develop Alberta's landmark coal policy. Currently we are working cooperatively with government and industry on guidelines for oil and gas activities and land management plans for various parts of Alberta.

Part of our job is to remain vigilant for threats to existing wilderness areas and other protected lands. Over the years we have successfully countered several development schemes for Willmore Wilderness Park, and rallied public opposition to many other poorly conceived proposals.

Our publishing activities include the publication of three popular and inexpensive guides to Alberta wildlands. One recent publication features eight of Alberta's outstanding wild rivers.

For teachers and groups, we have produced a 16-minute audio-visual program called "Why Wilderness?" that is available in videotape, 16-mm or slide-tape versions.

AWA services to the community are coordinated through our provincial office in Calgary. Through links to other groups, our executive director in Calgary keeps track of environmental concerns throughout Alberta and across Canada.

Appendix III

Scientific Names for Plants Referenced

Those interested in the flora of the Rocky Mountains should consult the floral keys:

Moss, E.H. 1983. *Flora of Alberta*. Sec. Ed. Revised by John G. Packer, University of Toronto Press, Toronto

Kuijt, Job. 1982. *A Flora of Waterton Lakes National Park*. University of Alberta Press, Edmonton.

Lichens, Mosses and Ferns

Feather moss   *Hylocomium splendens, Pleurazium schreberi; Ptilium crista-castrensis*
Grape Fern   *Botrychium lanceolatum*
Horsetail   *Equisetum sp.*
Lady Fern   *Athyrium filix-femina*
Old man's beard   *Usnea sp.*
Sphagnum moss   *Sphagnum sp.*

Trees and Shrubs

Alpine bearberry   *Arctostaphylos rubra*
Alpine fir   *Abies lasiocarpa*
Alpine larch   *Larix lyallii*
Aspen poplar   *Populus tremuloides*
Balsam poplar   *Populus balsamifera*
Bearberry   *Arctostaphylos uva-ursi*
Big sagebrush   *Artemisia tridentata*
Black spruce   *Picea mariana*
Bog birch   *Betula glandulosa* or *occidentalis*
Bog cranberry   *Vaccinium vitis-idaea*
Buffalo-berry   *Shepherdia canadensis*
Creeping juniper   *Juniperus horizontalis*
Crowberry   *Empetrum nigrum*

Deer brush   *Ceanothus velutinus*
Douglas fir   *Pseudotsuga menziesii*
Dwarf bilberry   *Vaccinium caespitosum*
Dwarf birch   *Betula pumila*
Dwarf willow   *Salix artica*
Engelmann spruce   *Picea engelmannii*
False huckleberry   *Menziesia ferruginea*
Green alder   *Alnus crispa*
Ground juniper   *Juniperus communis*
Grouse-berry   *Vaccinium scoparium*
Huckleberry   *Vaccinium membranaceum*
Juniper   *Juniperus communis, J. horizontalis*
Labrador tea   *Ledum groenlandicum*
Lapland rose-bay   *Rhododendron lapponicum*
Limber pine   *Pinus flexilis*
Lodgepole pine   *Pinus contorta*
Low bilberry   *Vaccinium myrtillus*
Mountain maple   *Acer glabrum*
Saskatoon   *Amelanchier alnifolia*
Shrubby cinquefoil   *Potentilla fruticosa*
Snow willow   *Salix nivalis*
Thimble berry   *Rubus parviforus*
Water birch   *Betula occidentalis*
Western red cedar   *Thuja plicata*
White spruce   *Picea glauca*
White-bark pine   *Pinus albicaulis*
White-flowered rhododendron   *Rhododendron albiflorum*
Wild gooseberry   *Ribes oxyacanthoides*
Wild rose   *Rosa acicularis*
Willow   *Salix sp.*

Grasses and Sedges

Alpine foxtail   *Alopecurus occidentalis*
Bluebunch wheat grass   *Agropyron spicatum*
Bluegrass   *Poa pattersonii* (Upper Oldman) *Poa sp.*
Brome   *Bromus sp.*

Fescue   *Festuca sp.*
Hairy wild rye   *Elymus innovatus*
Idaho fescue   *Festuca idahoensis*
June grass   *Koeleria macrantha*
Kobresia   *Kobresia sp.; Kobresia bellardii* (Elbow-Sheep)
Marsh reed grass   *Calamagrostis canadensis*
Northern awnless brome   *Bromus pumpellianus*
Parry oat grass   *Danthonia parryi*
Reed grass   *Calamagrostis sp.*
Rice grass   *Oryzopsis exigua*
Rough fescue   *Festuca scabrella*
Sedge   *Carex sp.*
Squirreltail   *Sitanion hystrix*
Wheat grass   *Agropyron sp.*

Flowering Plants

Alaska bog orchid   *Habenaria unalascensis*
Alpine arnica   *Arnica angustifolia*
Alpine cinquefoil   *Potentilla nivea*
Alpine forget-me-not   *Myosotis alpestris*
Alpine harebell   *Campanula uniflora*
Alpine poppy   *Papaver kluanensis*
Alum-root   *Heuchera parvifolia*
Arnica   *Arnica sp.*
Bear grass   *Xerophyllum tenax*
Blue camas   *Camassia quamash*
Bunchberry   *Cornus canadensis*
Buttercup   *Ranunculus sp.*
Calypso orchid   *Calypso bulbosa*
Chickweed   *Stellaria crispa* (Upper Oldman)
Cinquefoil   *Potentilla sp.*
Cliff Romanzoffia   *Romanzoffia stichensis*
Cow parsnip   *Heracleum lanatum*
Creeping grape   *Berberis repens*
Dwarf larkspur   *Delphinium bicolor*
Elephant head   *Pedicularis groenlandica*
Evergreen violet   *Viola orbiculata*
False Solomon's-seal   *Smilacina racemosa*

Fireweed   *Epilobium angustifolium, E. latifolium* (Burnt Timber); *Epilobium sp.*
Foam flower   *Tiarella unifoliata*
Gentian   *Gentiana glauca* (Whitegoat); *Gentiana sp.* (Upper Oldman)
Geyer's onion   *Allium geyeri*
Glacier lily   *Erythronium grandiflorum*
Globe-flower   *Trollius albiflorus*
Golden fleabane   *Erigeron aureus*
Golden bean   *Thermopsis rhombifolia*
Goldenrod   *Solidago multiradiata*
Grass-of-Parnasus   *Parnassia sp.*
Heart-leaved arnica   *Arnica cordifolia*
Hedysarum   *Hedysarum sp.*
Indian paintbrush   *Castilleja miniata* (Burnt Timber); *Castilleja sp.*
Jacob's-ladder   *Polemonium pulcherrimum*
Kitten-tails   *Besseya wyomingensis*
Larkspur   *Delphinium sp.*
Loco-weed   *Oxytropis sp.*
Lousewort   *Pedicularis artica, P. flammea* (Whitegoat); *Pedicularis sp.* (Ram-Whiterabbit)
Lyall's beard-tongue   *Penstemon lyallii*
Lyall's ironplant   *Saxifraga lyallii*
Mariposa lily   *Calochortus apiculatus*
Monkey-flower   *Mimulus floribundus*
Moss campion   *Silene acaulis*
Mountain avens   *Dryas hookeriana* (Burnt Timber, Upper Oldman, Elbow/Sheep); *Dryas integrifolia* (Whitegoat); *Dryas sp.*
Mountain lover   *Pachistima myrsinites*
Mountain marigold   *Caltha leptosepala*
One-flowered Clintonia   *Clintonia uniflora*
One-flowered wintergreen   *Moneses uniflora*
Perennial lupine   *Lupinus argenteus*
Pink wintergreen   *Pyrola asarifolia*
Prairie crocus   *Anemone patens*
Pucoon   *Lithospermum ruderale*
Purple alpine fleabane   *Erigeron purpuratus*
Purple heather   *Phyllodoce empetriformis*
Purple saxifrage   *Saxifraga occidentalis*
Ragwort   *Senecio sp.*

Rattlesnake plantain   *Goodyera oblongifolia*
Rock-jasmine   *Androsace chamaejasme*
Rocky Mountain willowherb   *Epilobium saximontanum*
Rose-root   *Tolmachevia integrifolia*
Saxifrage   *Saxifraga* sp.
Shooting star   *Dodecatheon conjugens*
Skunkweed   *Polemonium viscosum*
Sparrow's-egg slipper   *Cypripedium passerinum*
Spider plant   *Saxifraga flagellaris*

Star-flowered Solomon's seal   *Smilancia stellata*
Stonecrop   *Sedum lanceolatum* (Ram-Whiterabbit); *Sedum stenopetalum* (South Castle); *Sedum* sp.
Sweet cicely   *Osmorhiza chilensis* (Upper Oldman); *Osmorhiza occidentalis* (Whaleback)
Tall larkspur   *Delphinium glaucum*
Three-flowered avens   *Geum triflorum*
Townsendia   *Townsendia condensata*
Twin-flower   *Linnaea borealis*

Valerian   *Valeriana sitchensis*
Western anemone   *Anemone occidentalis*
White angelica   *Angelica arguta*
White camas   *Zigadenus elegans*
White dwarf fleabane   *Erigeron radicatus*
White mountain heather   *Cassiope tetragona*
White meadowsweet   *Spiraea betulifolia*
Wild chives   *Allium schoenoprasum*
Wild strawberry   *Fragaria* sp.
Wild onion   *Allium* sp.
Willow herb   *Epilobium saximontanum*

Wintergreen   *Pyrola* sp.
Wood lily   *Lilium philadelphicum*
Yellow angelica   *Angelica dawsonii*
Yellow balsam root   *Balsamorhiza sagittata*
Yellow columbine   *Aquilegia flavescens*
Yellow dryad   *Dryas drummondii*
Yellow heather   *Phyllodoce glanduliflora*
Yellow lady's-slipper   *Cypripedium calceolus*

Appendix IV

National Topographic Series Maps

WILD KAKWA   **1:50,000** 83E/13W, 83E/13E, 83E/14, 83L/3, 83L/4, 83L/5   **1:25,000** 83E, 83L

FOLDING MOUNTAIN   **1:50,000** 83F/4, 83F/5   **1:25,000** 83F

WHITE GOAT   **1:50,000** 83C/1, 83C/2, 83C/7, 83C/8, 83C/9, 83C/10   **1:25,000** 83C

RAM/WHITERABBIT   **1:50,000** 82N/16, 82O/12, 82O/13, 82O/14, 83B/4, 83C/1   **1:25,000** 82N, 82O, 83B, 83C

PANTHER CORNERS   **1:50,000** 82O/11, 82O/12   **1:25,000** 82O

BURNT TIMBER   **1:50,000** 82O/6, 82O/11, 82O/12   **1:25,000** 82O

SOUTH GHOST   **1:50,000** 82O/3, 82O/6   **1:25,000** 82O

UPPER KANANASKIS   **1:50,000** 82J/11   **1:25,000** 82J

ELBOW/SHEEP   **1:50,000** 82J/7, 82J/10, 82J/11, 82J/14, 82J/15, 82O/2, 82O/3   **1:25,000** 82J, 82O

NORTH PORCUPINE HILLS   **1:50,000** 82G/16, 82I/4, 82J/1   **1:25,000** 82G, 82I, 82J

WHALEBACK   **1:50,000** 82G/16, 82J/1   **1:25,000** 82G, 82J

UPPER OLDMAN   **1:50,000** 82G/15, 82G/16, 82J/2   **1:25,000** 82G, 82J

SOUTH CASTLE   **1:50,000** 82G/1, 82G/8, 82H/4   **1:25,000** 82G, 82H